W9-AOY-475

STENCILING MADE EASY

STENCILING MADE EASY

By Wanda Shipman

Illustrations by Dennis McDermott

Photographs by Stephen R. Swinburne

TAB BOOKS Inc.
Blue Ridge Summit, PA

FIRST EDITION
FIRST PRINTING

Copyright © 1989 by TAB BOOKS Inc.
Printed in the United States of America

Library of Congress Cataloging-in-Publication Data

Shipman, Wanda.
Stenciling made easy / by Wanda Shipman.
p. cm.
Includes index.
ISBN 0-8306-9167-7   ISBN 0-8306-3167-4 (pbk.)
1. Stencil work. I. Title.
TT270.S55 1989   89-4285
745.7'3—dc19   CIP

TAB BOOKS Inc. offers software for
sale. For information and a catalog,
please contact TAB Software Department,
Blue Ridge Summit, PA 17294-0850.

Questions regarding the content of this book
should be addressed to:

Reader Inquiry Branch
TAB BOOKS Inc.
Blue Ridge Summit, PA 17294-0214

Kimberly Tabor: Acquisitions Editor
Joanne M. Slike: Manuscript Editor
Katherine Brown: Production

Dedication

For Jennifer and Karen

Contents

Acknowledgments

Thanks to Christie Garneau of Stencil-Ease and to Robert Paul of Adele Bishop, who contributed the beautiful color photographs. A special thanks to Pat Estey, who created and stenciled many of the projects shown in the black-and-white photographs, and to Heather and Hayley Swinburne for their time and inspiration.

Introduction

FOR THE BEGINNER, a craft should be enjoyable, as headache-free as possible, and it should not demand a lengthy initiation into complicated means, methods, and materials before it can be enjoyed. Nor should it require a wealth of expensive supplies or equipment. But too often, even an easy and seemingly inexpensive craft like stenciling requires the beginner to memorize a catalog of technical terms and a list of do's and don'ts. Fear of "messing up" or of wasting precious time or materials can convince any would-be craftsperson that she just doesn't have the skills, funds, or patience to get involved.

The beginning stenciler who, like me, wants to find the most direct route to satisfying results can rest assured that she won't be led astray by appeals to buy unnecessary supplies or spend hours reading about the craft before enjoying it. She won't be asked to go about the task with the care and precision of a master craftsman in order to produce fine results, either. I don't have the desire to bury myself in abstractions before I attempt a craft, and I assume you don't, either.

For beginners—especially noncrafters who might be slightly intimidated by the connotation of the word "craftsman-ship"—perfection *is* possible. Every craft has several levels of expertise, and stenciling happens to be a very forgiving craft on every level. The supplies and materials made available by companies such as Adele Bishop and Stencil-Ease are designed to provide an easy route to perfection. For the first time ever stencilers can produce beautiful stenciling on a wide range of surfaces without making their own plates or mixing their own paints. All that a beginner really needs is a gentle boost in the right direction, with clear, easy-to-comprehend explanations about materials and techniques.

Unlike most stenciling books, this one doesn't include a section of make-your-own stencil plates. That's where many would-be stencilers stop before they even get started. You won't find a glossary of technical terms or a long list of necessary supplies, either. What you will find, I hope, is the inspiration and confidence to take a look at the scores of surfaces and materials in your home—walls, floors, fabrics, and furniture—and not just imagine how they might look transformed by stenciling, but transform them *yourself*.

Because stenciling can be addictive, you may find after several projects that you'd like to learn more about the craft. If this happens and you develop a desire to adapt and create original stencils or to tackle more advanced stenciling projects, there are two very good books that will help you on your way: *The Art of Decorative Stenciling*, by Adele Bishop and Cile Lord (Penguin Books), and *The Complete Book of Stencilcraft*, by JoAnne Day (Dover Publications). In both you'll find a selection of stencil plates to make yourself. Who knows? You might even begin enjoying the craft so much that you want to make a career of it.

❧ 1 ❧

A Brief History

IN A WAY, we can be glad that country stencilers a couple centuries ago couldn't afford wallpaper or rugs. These two floor coverings—standard decorating materials today—were simply too expensive for the average rural homeowner. Not only were they too costly, in most cases they were simply unavailable. Urban manufacturers did not have distributors for their products out in the countryside where most people still lived, and a trip into the city for anything more than essential goods would have been an unthinkable indulgence. Better to make do with what could be made at home with your own two hands.

Up until the Industrial Revolution, wallpaper and rugs were printed and woven by hand, and even after the advent of mechanization, they were, for the most part, luxuries only the "gentry" could afford. Still, the country dweller had to do something to cover bare plaster walls and rough-hewn floors. Contrary to popular belief, our ancestors—except perhaps for the Puritans—were not enamored of blacks and browns. They liked bright, strong color and plenty of it: on walls, floors, furniture, bed clothes, window coverings, and practically any other surface that would take

Opposite: Complementary stenciling colors and patterns can be used in an enormous variety of ways to decorate one room or several. Here, two different border stencils are used around a window and on the ceiling between beams, while a single pineapple spot stencil perks up a small wooden candle box hanging on the wall.

their simple home-concocted paints and dyes. Since early rural dwellers couldn't or wouldn't pay for the costly wall and floor coverings owned by the wealthy, they simulated them with paint, and in the process, invented a craft that many of us today find more aesthetically pleasing than the decorative items they were trying to copy.

Designs Used

At first, flowers, fruits, animals, and other coveted designs were painted on walls and floors freehand, a time-consuming practice with little chance of duplicating the precise patterns found on the real things. Then someone, somewhere, hit upon the idea of using stencils. With stencils, the designs could be repeated endlessly and uniformly—almost like the precise patterns found on wallpaper and rugs. Soon birds, flowers, fruits, and other favorite motifs climbed walls, hugged the ceiling and wainscotting, followed the lines of painted woodwork, and culminated in lavish displays of stencil work above fireplace mantels. Stenciling, in fact, could go places where wallpaper and rugs couldn't.

Floor Coverings

For 200 years or more, the standard floor covering in most rural homes in New England and elsewhere was either paint or, one step up, painted canvas "floor cloths." A favorite pattern for either was made up of checkered squares or diamonds of vivid red and yellow, or black and white. Large and stylized floral designs were popular, too. Painted canvas or boards may not have been as soft as carpeting beneath the feet, but they were a cinch to touch up when the paint wore off, and they could be made right on the premises using nothing more in the way of supplies and materials than what was found in the barn or the kitchen.

Colors

Stenciling colors were not the pastel hues we now associate with early country decor. Rural parlors and bed chambers of the eighteenth and nineteenth centuries were stenciled in vibrant reds, greens, yellows, and blues. Floors and walls were not the only surfaces that were decorated with stenciling. Picture and mirror frames, clock cases, wood and tin boxes of all sorts (salt boxes, document boxes, and trinket boxes, for example) chairs, chests, cupboards, bed coverlets, tablecloths, window shades, and other objects were painted with as much creative abandon as walls and floors. Virtually anything that didn't move—and that would take paint—was enlivened with colorful, stylized stenciling.

But walls and floors received the most attention, if only because they offered the largest canvas for the stenciler's creativity with paints and patterns. The supply of stenciling designs were never-ending. Favorite patterns taken directly from china, wallpaper, and other objects were used, but perhaps the most charming stencil designs evolved from actual living models—flowers, fruits, leaves, trees, birds, and barnyard animals—things commonly seen from the window and found around the homestead. While quilts, carved woodwork, and pottery provided instant inspiration, stenciling designs inspired by the stenciler's everyday life turned walls and other surfaces into a kind of scrapbook of the stenciler's home life. Pigs, cows, chickens, and other domestic animals "lived on" in their owner's imagination. A rooster, simply drawn and cut from a paper stencil, was very likely still alive and crowing out in the coop even as his image was being immortalized above the kitchen cookstove. But the stencil designs that held the most meaning for the rural stenciler symbolized the intangible: the weeping willow stood for eternity, the pineapple for hospitality, and the heart for joy—simple aspirations that gave meaning to a way of life devoid of many conveniences we take for granted today.

Professional Stencilers

Many a talented housewife did her own stenciling, just as she no doubt did her own knitting, quilting, rug-hooking, and basket-making before the age of mass production. But most big stenciling projects, such as floors and walls, were undertaken by the local pros. Itinerant stencilers, mostly men, as it happened, traveled from town to town hawking their artistic talents with paints and brushes. These rural artisans carried the simple tools of their trade with them wherever they went. Depending on the size and complexity of a stenciling project, the artisan would stay on with the family for a few days, or a week or more, until the job was done. Bed and board were his only pay. His crude stenciling tools and supplies—a few brushes, dry paint pigments, stencils of stiff paper or leather—fit into a box or case small enough to carry on top of his saddle.

Materials

The color of the dry organic pigments the stenciler used were usually determined not by the housewife's preference for a particular color scheme, but rather by the region in which the pigments were found. If the earth yielded red clay, then that's what the stenciler used. If the clay of the region was brown or yellow, then the stenciling would take on those colors. In addition to clay, brick dust, lamp black, and even blood were used as a color base for the stenciling. Skim milk from the kitchen turned them all into paint. The natural colors of a region in which a stenciler worked might determine the colors and patterns (for the stenciler carried a limited array of stencil patterns with him) for miles around. When his job was finished in one house, the itinerant stenciler simply packed his pigments, brushes, and stencils and moved onto the next set of bare walls and floors.

A large but simple two-color spot stencil from a farmhouse in Norwich, Vermont.

In spite of the limitations of early stenciling materials and the standard hit-and-run method of stenciling, the decorative results were almost always a monumental improvement over bare plaster and floorboards. But like most folk art, primitive stenciling was limited by the materials available to the stenciler and the skills of the craftsman. Flowers, animals, and other objects could not be rendered realistically because the stencil plates would be too complicated and time-consuming to use. At any rate, there were simply not enough colors available to duplicate the subtle hues found in the real things. Later, skilled craftsmen like Seth Thomas and Lambert Hitchcock would refine the craft to an art form with their intricate stencilwork on clock cases and chairs; however, they would have scores of talented artisans working for them. The country artisan was far more limited by the time and materials at his disposal.

Stenciling Today

Yet those very limitations gave the craft the simple charm that many of us yearn for today. Despite the availability of intricately patterned wallpaper and rugs, homeowners today—rural and urban alike—want to duplicate the primitive look of early country stenciling. So we've come full circle! We are, however, not saddled with the primitive stenciling materials and methods used a century or two ago. Stenciling, like most other old-time crafts, has long since been refined to near perfection.

Today's stenciling materials allow stencilers to render designs as intricate as those of a Thomas or a Hitchcock. The range of stenciling patterns and paints available to today's stenciler far exceeds the simple pigments, brushes, and paper stencils found in the itinerant country stenciler's humble workbox. Yet we can emulate the rustic, hand-wrought look of early stenciling with the simple two-toned heart, flower, bird, or fruit motifs that the country homeowner cherished so much. In fact, the whole point of country stenciling today is to do just that, right down to the primitive, stylized patterns and uneven paint application. And why not? Now that certain furnishings have become as predictable and standard as aluminum siding, many of us once again are happy to substitute old-fashioned, hand-done country graphics for expensive wallpaper and carpeting.

❦ 2 ❧

Tools of
the Craft

STENCILING is a forgiving craft. Those who can't draw, paint, sew, weave, carve, or sculpt (and I count myself among this large group) can, with confidence and a little preparation, create beautiful country graphics for their walls, floors, and furnishings. You do not need a steady hand or a practiced eye to transform dull, ordinary rooms or objects into visual delights of personal style and warmth. Nor do you need to spend all day at an artist's supply store emptying your pockets on paints, tools, special paper, and other materials that you may use only once, then pack away in frustration.

With the wealth of ready-to-use stenciling supplies now available in stenciling shops, department stores, drug stores, and even artist's supply stores, you can "countrify" your home with the skill of an old-time artisan. And you can do it without investing hours gathering and preparing materials or practicing the craft. You can, in fact, stencil a whole room in the time it once took to prepare a simple stencil plate.

Because much, if not all, of the time-consuming prep work of traditional stenciling is eliminated for modern-day stencilers, we can pour all of our time, effort, and creativity into the "business end" of the craft: painting pictures onto surfaces. While skipping the mundane processes—finding a suitable pattern, drawing it, transferring it and cutting it out, mixing the paints, and so forth—we can busy ourselves with stenciling's many decorative possibilities. Never has the craft been so easy to master, or the results so instantly rewarding, as they are today.

To those who might object to "taking the easy route," I can only respond that a few people might miss all the preparatory steps involved in traditional stenciling, every agonizing inch of the way. It is true that mastering a craft in its entirety may make someone more of an artisan than a crafter; but in stenciling, the results won't necessarily be better. The stenciler who researches, draws, transfers, and cuts out her own stenciling patterns may experience some gratification that the rest of us can't know. On the other hand, the rest of us won't know (or possibly care) whether the charming border stenciled around a friend's dining room walls was the result of hours of prestenciling labor.

If you plan to go into the business of stenciling full-time, you may want to learn the craft inside and out. But if your aim is to enjoy a pleasant afternoon transforming a dull room or a piece of furniture and still have time to prepare dinner for guests that evening, my guess is that you'll be delighted to take advantage of the range and quality of all the manufactured stenciling supplies available to the beginning stenciler. If you want to have the baby's nursery stenciled in ducks or elephants in time for his or her arrival, you probably will not want to spend time tracing and cutting out stencil patters, especially if you only have a month or two to go before the main event. For a few dollars and a few hours, you can

A well-stocked stencil shop will supply everything the first-time stenciler needs: brushes, textile and japan paints, stencil plates, books, and a wealth of ideas in prestenciled objects. This shop, owned and operated by Pat Estey of Manchester, Vermont, carries stencil patterns produced by major stenciling manufacturers, as well as her own custom designs.

finish the nursery while the purist is still drawing the duck or elephant onto graph paper.

Stenciling is so easy, in fact, that you might be tempted to stop by a stenciling shop, pick up a few paints, a couple of brushes, and a stencil or two and throw yourself into it without further ado. I say you could do this because I've done it—with so-so results. I discovered after the second or third project, however, that I would have appreciated a few tips before I plunged into my first project. Some people (not I) have an innate talent with crafts and can produce wonderful results on their first attempt. For example, my younger sister decided that she would give a mirror in her bedroom one last chance before throwing it away. Having never stenciled before, she picked up some japan paints and a floral stencil plate and went to work on it. The results were beautiful, so much so that she decided to go on to stencil the walls in her family room. But she said the mirror frame took at least an hour because she had to work out the basic stenciling technicalities as she stenciled: applying the paint properly, turning corners, and keeping the stencil plate firmly in

Pat Estey prepares to stencil one of the many small wooden objects she sells in her shop. She also stencils and sells wall-hangings, clothing, and other stenciled fabrics.

place. Where most people would have abandoned the project, she kept going, teaching herself the hard way before tackling the much larger wall-stenciling project downstairs. That project took just a little longer than the mirror stenciling did.

So, what are these miracle stenciling materials awaiting the first-time stenciler? Here they are, all three or four of them, and a word about how and why each works so well.

Paints

Traditional stencilers of the past had, at most, three or four colors to work with at a time. To their dry pigments they added skim milk, working and reworking the color combinations until they reached the desired hue and consistency for stenciling. Needless to say, it took a certain amount of experience to get consistently good results, and even then, the stenciler might run out of pigment, milk, or both, and have to improvise or stop working. Today, stencilers can easily produce an infinite array of colors for stenciling: everything from the subtlest cornflower blue, rose pink, or apple green, to the deepest barn red or olive green. Premixed paints, both water-soluble and oil-based, come packed in handy 1- or 2-ounce jars and cans, each with enough pigment to stencil a small neighborhood of houses. The individual paints are ready to use straight from their containers, or they can be mixed together to create custom colors true enough to match virtually any shade.

You'll find that by custom-mixing your own paint colors, you can create a stenciling scheme that is truly individual. Unless your furnishings are extremely unusual in color, you will have little trouble finding stencil paints to complement them. But you can go one step further by *precisely* matching stenciling paints to colors already found in your home—not only customizing your stenciling scheme to your particular color scheme, but virtually guaranteeing that you won't see your stenciling colors in someone else's home. Custom-mixing stencil paints is an easy way to get more stenciling mileage out of a few basic paint colors, as well as add a measure of personal creativity to the craft. Try matching stenciling colors to colors found in curtains, lamp shades, upholstery, rugs, ceramics, and other furnishings, and you may find that even the scores of "standard" stenciling paint colors are too limited for your imagination.

One important, perhaps the most important, quality of these paints is their fast-drying ability. If they didn't dry quickly on contact, your stenciling efforts would be sorry indeed. Instead of being pleasurable, stenciling would be a time-consuming chore. Not only would the wet paint smear and run beneath the stencil pattern, it would take hours to finish one wall. Imagine waiting a day or two before putting on the second stencil plate for a different color. Small wonder early stencilers limited their stencil patterns to one or two colors.

Textile paint. Water-soluble textile paint, sometimes called acrylic paint, is a pleasure to use. In fact, many stencilers limit their stenciling projects to those surfaces that can take this paint because it is so easy to use and to clean up. Unlike oil-based japan paint, it does not need to be thinned with turpentine. You also don't have to clean tools and materials—brushes, plates, work surfaces, and containers—with turpentine or mineral spirits. Water-based textile paint is perfect for all types of dull surfaces, from walls to small wooden pieces to fabrics. (In fact, this is *the* paint for stenciling fabrics.) It produces stenciling that is thin yet opaque in appearance (as though it was painted on with brick dust and skim milk), permanent yet washable. Unlike the japan paint described below, textile paint is used straight from the container and is cleaned up with simple soap and water—something that recommends it especially highly to beginning stencilers. When you are just beginning to get the hang of holding a brush, positioning the stencil, and applying the paint, you shouldn't have to worry about the mess. The more you can concentrate on technique, the better your early stenciling efforts will be. Textile paint is especially well-suited to "country" stenciling because it has a wonderfully soft, translucent quality when applied to dull surfaces. Imagine the grain of a dark wood showing through soft, pastel stenciling.

Water-based textile, or acrylic, paints are used on dull surfaces such as flat-painted walls, unfinished wood, and fabrics. It is the easiest stencil paint to use because it does not require thinning with turpentine and cleans up easily with simple soap and water.

Japan paint. Oil-based japan paint is a little trickier to work with than water-soluble textile paint, but it produces superior results on hard, glossy surfaces that will not take textile stenciling paint. Japan paint adheres well to these surfaces, and to any surface (except fabric) where you want a bit more coverage and depth of color. This is especially important on walls and furniture, for example, that are painted a dark, glossy color. Where textile paint will "float" around on this kind of surface rather than sticking to it, japan paint will adhere well. This is the paint you should use on most walls, furniture, and metals.

Oil-based japan paint produces deep, vivid stenciling on hard surfaces such as most walls, finished wood, tinware, and other glossy or semiglossy surfaces. It is thinned with turpentine before use and is cleaned up with turpentine or mineral spirits.

As mentioned earlier, japan paint must be thinned with turpentine and cleaned up with turpentine or mineral spirits, but it is well worth the extra work if you want to stencil beautifully clean-looking, durable patterns on certain surfaces. Japan paint might also be your choice for tiny, intricate stenciling because it is easier to achieve a sharp outline than with textile paint, which by its very nature is "soft" in appearance. Japan paints can also be custom-mixed to produce a wide range of light and dark colors.

Brushes

Stencil brushes give stenciling its special hand-done quality. Stencil brushes are round and stiff-bristled, and allow you to paint the stencil pattern in broad strokes, filling the pattern in and shading it simultaneously before the paint dries. The bristles of a stencil brush are round and are cut perfectly flat across the base. When applying the paint, you should hold the brush straight down, not at an angle like most other paint brushes.

With a few circular strokes, a pattern can be quickly and easily shaded from dark to light, a technique that gives good stenciling its unmistakable three-dimensional quality. Stencil brushes come in different sizes: small-girthed brushes are used to paint in the small details of a stencil pattern, while larger ones take care of a pattern's broad areas. Good-quality stencil brushes are recommended, as well as a different brush for each color used in a particular stencil pattern. A brush for each color will not only keep the paint colors from getting mixed together, it will also make the project go much faster because you won't have to stop to clean the brush before applying the next color. As you can see, quick brush strokes and fast-drying paints work together to allow the stenciler to produce a repetitive design on a large surface in the shortest amount of time.

Stencil Plates

Plastic stencil plates are remarkable little vehicles for creative expression. With just a couple of strips of plastic you can personalize a whole room and its furnishings with virtually any motif you have in mind, whether it is a lifelike floral pattern for a formal dining room, or a primitive border of sheep, cows, and other barnyard animals for the baby's room. For quick, easy, and inexpensive decorating, there is nothing quite like stenciling to bring plain, quiet surfaces alive with personality and color.

A stencil (the tool and its results claim the same name) is composed of one, two, three, or even ten plates, depending upon the intricacy of the pattern, the number of colors it contains, and the industry of the stenciler. Imagine a two-color stencil pattern

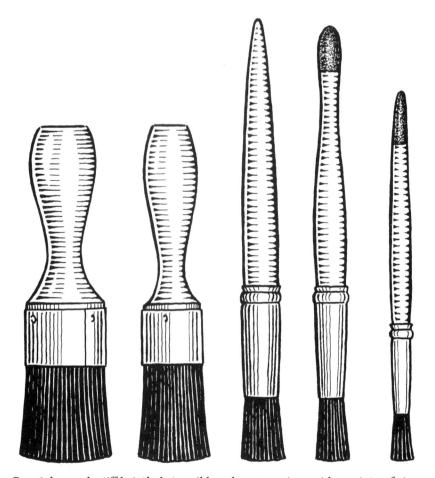

Special round, stiff-bristled stencil brushes come in a wide variety of sizes. The smallest are used to fill in tiny portions of a stencil pattern, while the largest brushes are used to fill in large stencil patterns with a few broad strokes. Always use a separate brush for each paint color, whether you are using water-based textile paint or oil-based japan paint.

composed of a continuous vine-and-berry design. The first plate (plate 1) will have the vine part of the pattern cut out, while the second plate (plate 2) will have only the berries cut out. The stencil paint is first brushed onto the cutout sections of the vine. Once the green vine is stenciled onto the wall, floor, or other surface, the second plate (the berries) is held over the impression of the vine, and the second color (red or blue) is stenciled in. When both plates of the vine-and-berry pattern are stenciled onto the surface, the whole pattern and its two major parts (vine and berries) will appear in their correct relations to one another, completing the two-color "picture" that neither of the two plates can produce alone.

Using Stencils

Painting with stencils is *almost* like painting by numbers, but not quite. While a manufacturer may suggest which colors to use with a given stencil pattern, any number of different color combinations can be used, depending on: 1. the stenciler's personal color preferences; 2. what colors already exist in a room; or 3. what paints you already have on hand. Stenciling allows a great deal of flexibility in paint choices as well as their application. You might want to apply the paint heavily on small stencil patterns, especially if the surface to be stenciled is dark, or apply lightly on large, primitive patterns that might overwhelm a room if stenciled too dark. The degree of shading you use will, again, depend on the quality of the stenciled surface and the style of the stencil pattern or room. Larger stencil patterns are easier to shade, and almost fade into the woodwork, if subtle colors are used. But because of their greater size, they remain prominent. Small patterns, if shaded too delicately, would almost disappear, so you will want to stencil them in more vibrant colors, without too much shading. When you consider the intuitive decisions that you'll have to make before choosing the colors of your paint and how to apply it, you realize that stenciling is not "by-the-number."

Using a stencil, on the other hand, is as easy as drawing a pencil line using a ruler. By using simple register or guide marks printed on each stencil plate, you can line up each plate precisely with the other plates, as well as with the stenciling itself. So long as you take care to keep the right side of the plate facing outwards (usually the shiny side), it is easy to align the plate you are working with over the stenciling produced by an earlier plate.

Here's how it works. When stenciling virgin walls or other surfaces, the first part of the pattern (plate 1) must be stenciled on. Simply hold border stencils flush against a vertical or horizontal edge, such as the baseboard or a corner where two walls meet. Then hold a spot stencil against the center of the surface, or wherever you've chosen to place it, using an "X" or other centering mark you've penciled on as a guide. Once you've stenciled in the pattern on plate 1, place plate 2 over the pattern. The cutout portions of the pattern on plate 2 should fall on blank space between the unstenciled portions of plate 1. The stenciling produced by plate 1 will line up with register marks on plate 2 to show you exactly where to position plate 2 for stenciling. On border stencils, register marks at either end of the plates will show you where to position a plate in order to continue the border design.

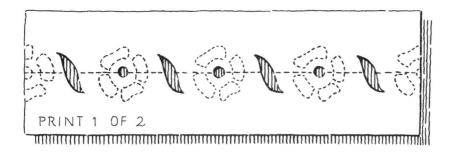

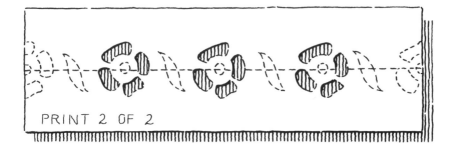

A complete stencil pattern is filled in by using two or more plates. Each plate represents one portion and one color of the pattern. Here, plate 1 of the two-color border stencil has only the small geometric shape and center of the flowers cut out. Plate 2 has only the flower petals cut out. When combined, the plates produce the whole pattern in two colors.

Using these two sets of register marks on a border stencil as a guide, you can move swiftly along, filling in the next empty space at baseboard or ceiling with stenciling until you've stenciled the entire perimeter of a room. Then, with stencil plate 2, you can go back to the beginning and start stenciling in the second portion of the pattern on top of the first border, moving just as quickly and efficiently as you did with plate 1. Subsequent plates and portions of the same pattern can be filled in just as easily and quickly, so that an average-size room can be stenciled with a two- or three-color pattern within a very short time. The paint will dry faster than you can move the stencil along the wall.

Good paints and brushes are important, but clear, well-cut stencil plates are essential. In the past, stencilers made their stencil plates out of stiff, opaque paper that tended to last only a few sessions with the brush and paint before falling apart. Imagine trying to stencil a three-part pattern without being able to see the stenciling produced by the first stencil plate. Today's see-through plastic stencils, precut, or drawn and ready to be cut out by hand, make it much simpler to see what you are doing and to do it quickly. And plastic stencils last virtually forever. They do not tear or fall apart when used with either oil-based or water-soluble paints, and they bend easily into tight places such as corners. On the other hand, a paper stencil, once bent to accommodate a corner or other tight area, might have to be discarded because it will never lie flat again. Like stencil paints and brushes, manufactured stencils come in a bewildering array of patterns and sizes, each of which can be used in its entirety, in sections, or in combination with other stencil patterns. Compared to the materials used a century ago, modern stenciling supplies make the craft as easy as falling off the veritable log.

Other Supplies

The inevitable few remaining supplies you'll need to assemble before embarking on your first stenciling project are probably already on hand: masking tape to hold the stencil plate to the surface, paper towels to blot off excess paint before brushing it on the stencil, a couple of brown grocery bags for discarded materials, some blank white paper that you can use to make a few ''test runs''

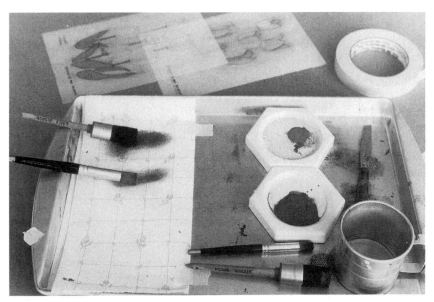

The basic stenciler's kit: stencil plates, brushes, paint, turpentine, masking tape, paper towels, and a cookie sheet to hold it all.

before stenciling, turpentine if you're using japan paint, coffee cans for cleaning brushes used with japan paint, a cookie sheet or similar tray on which to hold everything, and a chair or a stool to help you reach the top of the wall.

You can forget the cutting board, knives and blades, drawing pens, tracing paper, graph paper, T-square, artists' paints, metallic powders, and any and all technical jargon such as "fret," "frieze," and "mitering." We will not "enlarge," "reduce," or "transfer" stencil patterns, nor will we "stipple," "sponge," or "spray" them on (although many beginning stencilers, in the heat of stenciling, may decide to graduate to the loftier levels of the craft). For now, however, we'll spend more time choosing colors, patterns, and surfaces than we will memorizing unmemorable terminology and techniques. With all due respect to master stencilers of past and present, while we are lucky to have the best of their designs preserved in modern stencils, we are equally fortunate that the most difficult and time-consuming aspects of the craft need no longer be mastered by the rest of us in order to create hand-stenciled decorations of the same high quality.

❧ 3 ❧

Supplies & Techniques

STENCILS have been made from anything thin and flexible enough to be held against a smooth surface—everything from paper and leather to brass and vinyl. They have been used to stencil walls, floors, store signs, even stagecoach doors, and all will work. But clear, flexible plastic is the material found in most modern stenciling kits. Paper was once the most common type of stencil plate, and it is still used by professional stencilers practiced enough at their craft to create original designs, adapt nonstencil patterns for one-of-a-kind projects, or make on-the-spot variations.

But for the beginning stenciler, paper stencils have too many drawbacks. For one thing, paper stencils have a brief life span. Stencil paints are hard to remove from paper, and paper stencils just can't stand up as well as plastic under frequent use. Needless to say, it is difficult to see through paper stencils, making intricate, multi-plate stenciling difficult to use. Some large stenciling projects may even require you to use several sets of paper stencils for one pattern, as it is easier to recut torn, creased, or paint-gunked paper stencils than use them again. In other words, paper is largely why stencil manufacturers started producing clear, cleanable, reusable plastic stencils for the nonprofessional.

Plastic allows you to stack two or three stencil plates atop each other like playing cards, without losing sight of the pattern you drew with the first plate. Plastic stencils allow you to see what you're doing to the surface of the wall, curtain, rug, or chest *as you stencil*. Plastic stencils bend easily to fit into corners or around curved surfaces and spring back to life afterward when you need to use them to stencil the rest of the wall. And plastic stencils can take almost unlimited use (or abuse) from paints, brushes, and cleansers and still be in good shape for the next long project. You can easily wipe paint off them with soap and water or mineral spirits, and unless you scrub a plastic stencil with the dedication of a charwoman, the pattern will not tear or stretch out of shape. The plastic stencil you use on your living room walls today can be used in your dining room next week or in the bedroom next year. If a plastic stencil does tear while you are using it, simply patch it up with transparent tape—even if you are in the middle of a project.

While I prefer to use precut stencils, thus pushing the notion of convenience to its utmost limits, many good patterns can only be found in an uncut state. Having to cut out one of these stencils doesn't compare at all to the effort that goes into transferring, registering, and cutting out your own design, of course. It simply means that you must perform one more step before you can begin stenciling: cutting out the pattern already drawn and registered on the surface of each plate. To do this, you must trace around the pattern with a sharp X-acto knife, using a piece of glass as a cutting surface. The trick is to swivel the stencil plate as you hold the blade's edge still. It does take a little practice, and you will have to take care not to stray from the outline of the pattern, but if you do it carefully, you should have no trouble. If you can, though, use a precut stencil for your first project. You should have little trouble finding one that you like, and it will make things that much simpler and more enjoyable.

Anatomy of a Stencil

The anatomy of a stencil is what helps the craft turn out nearly perfect on the first try, no matter how complicated a pattern. "Bridges" of uncut plastic between each element of a pattern (flower petals or bird feathers, for example) are what physically hold the pattern in place. Each cutout petal or feather is isolated from the others until the separate stencil plates gradually fill in the spaces around all of the elements. After the second, third, or fourth stencil plate, a whole rose or an entire rooster will appear. The separate plates of pattern not only allow you to use separate colors, they also fill in the various elements of the pattern itself.

Take a look at a stencil plate and you'll see that without those bridges of space surrounding each element, you'd have either the barest outline of a rose or a funny-looking hole, depending on your powers of imagination. The need to carefully arrange those bridges is one of the things that makes adapting and drawing your own stencil patterns so difficult and time-consuming. Stencilers who make their own plates have to figure out where to put the bridges of space in order to keep the pattern from literally falling apart.

Register marks make sense as soon as you hold a stack of stencil plates together in the right order (the separate plates are always marked plate 1, plate 2, plate 3, and so forth). The marks, usually dashes, indicate where each plate lines up over the one below it, showing you exactly where the red or blue berries in plate 2 will go in relation to the green leaves and vine of plate 1. Register marks also show you where to pick up a border stencil at the last impression, even if you stopped working on it the day before. Without register marks to show you where to position a plate in relation

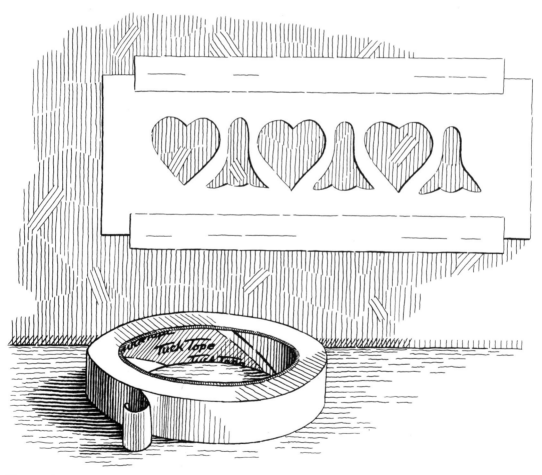

Uncut "bridges" of plastic surrounding the cutout portions of a stencil pattern actually hold the pattern's shape together. Here, a simple one-color stencil pattern is held firmly in place on the surface to be stenciled with masking tape.

to the last impression you made with it, it would be impossible to stencil around a ceiling using a 10-inch-long border stencil. You would need a stencil as long as the perimeter of the whole room.

Borders and Spots

"Border" and "spot" stencils will make up our limited repertoire of stencil types. There are different names for different types of border stencils and different names for different types of spot stencils. But why not keep the terminology simple? Borders and spots are the two basic types of stencils needed to do most stenciling jobs. And all you really need to remember is that border stencils are used repetitively, or continuously, along horizontal and vertical edges (such as the tops and bottoms of walls and the sides of doors and windows), while spot stencils are used alone (in the center panel of a chest or drawer) or in sequence (going up a stairwell, perhaps, or lined up on a wall below wainscotting). Border stencils are generally long and narrow, while spot stencils are usually large and square.

As the name implies, border stencils are used to "border" the vertical and horizontal edges of surfaces such as walls, floors, windows, doors, and any object or space with definite boundaries that can be framed with an uninterrupted line of stenciling. Border stencils do much to enliven broad, plain walls and define small, uninteresting windows and other openings. A room with little architectural interest takes on more depth and definition when it is enclosed or outlined with lines of shape and color. Suddenly the windows don't look quite so small or the door so stark.

Spot stencils, on the other hand, are generally used *within* those borders, or alone at various intervals within border stenciling. Just as border stenciling helps to outline and to define bland spaces, spot stenciling helps to fill it up. The center of door panels and drawer fronts are good places for spot stencils. So are stair risers and featureless (and often furnitureless) stairwells. Think of spot stencils as "pictures" and border stencils as "frames" and you'll get a general and useful idea of their two different functions when it comes time to decorate those lifeless spaces in your home.

Border stencils are often made up of a series of geometric shapes, flowers, leaves, fruits, or animals. Spots are usually made up of one subject: a bird (the peacock and bird of paradise, both highly symbolic, by the way, are two common examples), a basket of flowers, an arrangement of fruit, a single-piece-of fruit (a pineapple, for instance), people, and even large, detailed scenes. Spot stencils work well when framed either by the outside edges of an object itself (door, chest, rug, tablecloth, or bedspread) or by border stenciling in a coordinating design and colors. Spot stencils can be anywhere from a couple of inches to more than a foot in size, while border stencils range from less than a couple of inches to more than a foot in height and three or four times that in length.

The two types of stencils are also interchangeable. You can use spot stencils repetitively along the top of a wall, up a stairwell, or below wainscotting (or faux wainscotting created by a border stencil) as easily as you can use a portion of a large or small border stencil as a spot stencil for small objects such as stationery, a tin cup, or a chair back. You can also use one portion of a border stencil—the narrow border that is frequently found as part of the pattern in a very large border stencil—to complement the larger design.

You might, for example, use a large border around the perimeter of a room and a small portion of that border around the perimeter of a lampshade. And although you can use a spot stencil repetitively as you would a border stencil, you will have to mark off on the surface where each spot will go so the border comes out evenly spaced. Finally, you can mix spots and borders. You might interrupt your main border stenciling at various well-thought-out intervals, such as at the corners and at wide intervals along walls, with large spot stencils. This will not only help fill up space on large walls but will provide an instant solution to the sometimes tricky problem of turning corners, which we'll address later.

Using the Brush

Because of its shape, a stencil brush is easy to use correctly. Stencil brushes are round, chubby, stiff-bristled affairs that are cut flat across at the business end. This shape makes it unlikely that anyone would try to use a stencil brush as they would a conventional paintbrush. In fact, stencil brushes are closer to scrub brushes in design and use, and they are ideally suited to their medium—the stencil paint. Because stencil paint must go onto the surface nearly dry (so it can dry fast, for one thing, and not smudge or run), it must be virtually *rubbed* onto the stencil plate. The round shape of the stencil brush encourages this kind of application, and it also encourages the stenciler to apply the paint in the correct *circular* motion, which gives stenciling its shaded, translucent quality. When applying paint in a circular fashion you simultaneously shade the paint as you brush it on.

Stencil brushes come in small, medium, and large sizes. The smallest stencil brushes (about the width of an ordinary pencil) are used to stencil in tiny portions of a pattern and to stencil very narrow borders. The largest stencil brushes (more than an inch across) allow you to lay on the paint quickly and easily in large areas and to shade the paint before it dries. Because stenciling goes so

Borders and spots can be used in a variety of ways to complement one another and to solve "tactical" problems, such as turning corners. Here, a fan-shaped spot stencil is combined with two different border stencils, one of which does not complement the spot stencil. The geometric border would work well with the spot stencil, but the floral border would look mismatched. Spot stencils are usually used alone, while border stencils are used to produce repetition of the same pattern along horizontal and vertical edges such as the tops and sides of walls.

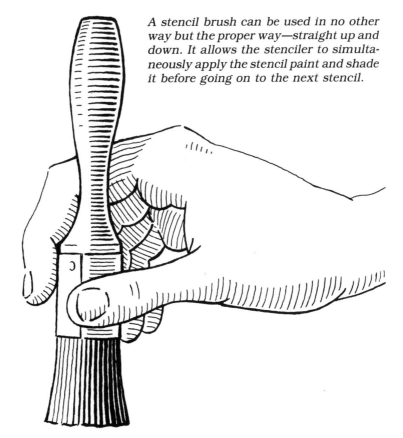

A stencil brush can be used in no other way but the proper way—straight up and down. It allows the stenciler to simultaneously apply the stencil paint and shade it before going on to the next stencil.

quickly, a separate brush is always used for each color, otherwise, you'd lose valuable time cleaning the brush and waiting for it to dry before going onto the next color. For your first job, three brushes of various sizes will probably suffice unless you are working with a large spot stencil of more than three different colors—something I wouldn't advise for a first-time stenciler, especially if you are using japan paint.

Don't limit yourself to one or two brushes, even on your first project. At two or three dollars each, they are inexpensive enough to stock up on. And again, in the time it would take to clean and dry a brush between paint colors—especially if you are using an oil-based, japan paint, which must be cleaned with mineral spirits—you could stencil an entire room. Be sure to reserve separate brushes for the two types of paint, water-based and oil-based, because traces of oil may be left on a brush used with japan paint, making it difficult to clean up with water and soap. So buy enough brushes—you'll be glad you did.

Stenciling Technique

By making a few trial runs with stencil, brush, and paint on blank white paper, you'll not only get a feel for how to hold the brush and how much paint to apply, you'll also give yourself a chance to see how you like the results before committing the stenciling to a permanent surface. Blank white copier paper makes an excellent testing ground for your stenciling. You can practice stenciling until you feel you've mastered all the right moves (there are 500 sheets of paper per ream, remember) and can use those practice stencils to give yourself a preview of the finished work by taping them in place on the surface to be stenciled. Colors that may look right in the container or even on the brush may look too light or dark on the final surface. A blue that looks subtle enough in a tiny can or jar may look glaring when used in a large border running the whole length of a room. Or a color that seems vivid on the label may not show up enough on a small stencil or a dark surface. So use these test stencils to avoid any unpleasant surprises. If, for some reason, the pattern or colors you've chosen for the kitchen walls turn out to be deadly (maybe you didn't take the avocado refrigerator into account when you chose them), all you will have lost is a little time, paint, paper, and tape.

The rule of thumb for paint application is this: be as stingy with it as possible. Just barely tip the ends of the brush into the paint and immediately wipe the bristles off on a folded paper towel or rag as though you were trying to get *rid* of the paint. *Never* dip the brush in as though you were painting the whole wall, for that's probably how much paint you would need to stencil the whole wall. The idea is to wipe off most of the paint *before* you touch the brush to the stencil plate. This way you will probably succeed in applying just

Test stencils not only allow you to test colors and patterns before using them, they also give you a feel for the right paint consistency. Here, three impressions of the same stencil pattern carry different amounts of paint. The one that came out "just right" is in the center.

the right amount of paint to produce a clear, nicely shaded, sharp-edged stencil that does not run under the plate, smudge when you lift the plate, or take more than a few heartbeats to dry. If you do dunk that brush into the paint, you'll soon see the error of your move. The paint will—I promise—swim on the surface and, worse, ooze beneath the edge of the pattern, a place where it should never be allowed to go. The result will be a wet Rorschach open to only one interpretation: you used too much paint!

The only way to "fix" faulty stenciling is to wipe it off completely and start again. On the other hand, in the unlikely event that you use too little paint, you will merely have to add a bit more until the stencil pattern has enough coverage. Try to apply the same amount of paint each "repeat" of a border stencil, too. Some color variation will be fine, even desirable, because stenciling should look uneven in tone. It should not duplicate the uniformity of wallpaper patterns. But if the paint is too uneven, if a border goes from light to dark and back again, it will be distracting. This shouldn't be too much of a problem if you have practiced on paper before going for the wall, however. Just remember, when using stencil paint it is always better to err on the side of stinginess. Always prefer to add paint rather than take it away.

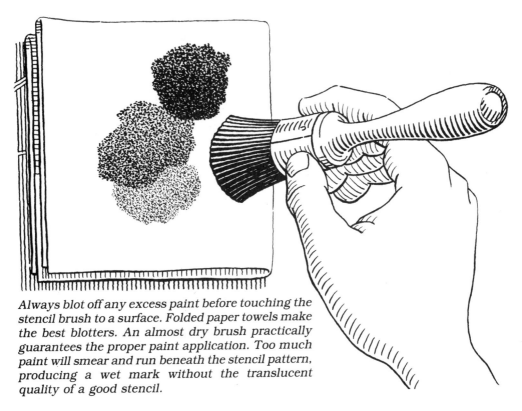

Always blot off any excess paint before touching the stencil brush to a surface. Folded paper towels make the best blotters. An almost dry brush practically guarantees the proper paint application. Too much paint will smear and run beneath the stencil pattern, producing a wet mark without the translucent quality of a good stencil.

Once beginners learn that the right amount of stencil paint means almost none, they find that shading with the paint is as easy as applying it—because it is almost the same thing. It is impossible to shade at all if the brush is full of paint, but when the right amount and consistency is used, shading occurs automatically. To shade in a stencil pattern move the brush in broad, circular motions from the edges of the pattern toward the center. As you move the brush inward, it will become drier, less paint will be transferred to the surface, and *voila*— the stenciling is shaded from dark at the edges, to light in the center. The dark, crisp edges will help "lift" the stenciling from the surface while the lighter center will give it a somewhat three-dimensional quality that is translucent at the same time. Of course, the principle works when shading from right to left, or from top to bottom, too. Here's another reason to do several test stencils on paper. Depending on the pattern, you may want shade for the illusion of depth in a particular area, just as you would when painting a picture. When using a large, repetitive border you will also want to shade each "repeat" pattern in the same place to give the border consistency. In other words, you will want all of your teddy bears to be shaded light-to-dark in roughly the same place.

Shading

To shade properly and consistently, simply start rubbing the paint onto the stencil where you want the pattern to be darkest, working the paint into (and off of) the portion of the stenciling that you want to be the lightest. Start painting each repeat in the same place and the shading will come out the same for each. Attention to shading is what gives stenciling its hand-done look. If stenciling paint were applied thickly or uniformly, especially on large patterns, the stenciling would look printed, rather than hand-painted.

Oil-based japan paints and water-soluble textile paints are both applied in the same manner—almost dry and in circular, shading motions. However, as I mentioned in Chapter 2, there are a few differences between the two paints. Japan paint is always used on hard, shiny surfaces such as walls, floors, and furniture. It adheres to these surfaces the way that water-based paints cannot. Also, japan paint must be thinned to the right consistency and depth of color with turpentine and cleaned up with turpentine or mineral spirits (which is much cheaper and worth buying just for cleaning up your brushes, stencils, and fingers).

Textile paint is always used on fabrics and on dull surfaces such as small, unfinished or stained wooden pieces, and wall painted in flat paint. While japan paint is used for its adherence and depth of coverage (especially when the stenciling must compete with a vividly colored background), textile paint produces a "thin" stencil

Good shading can give stenciling a translucent, nearly three-dimensional quality. Notice how the abstract flowers in this spot stencil are shaded from dark to light, while the smaller petals and geometrics are almost solid in tone. The crisp outlines result from using the right paint consistency: almost dry.

that allows the surface to show through easily. Textile paint is used directly from the container and cleans up with soap and water. For these reasons textile paint is an excellent paint for beginners, and many experienced stencilers prefer to use it whenever they can, even to the extent of stenciling only surfaces that will take this water-based paint.

Both paints can be mixed to produce custom shades, making it unnecessary to stock up on several shades of either type of paint. In fact, you should never buy more stencil paints than you will need for one project. When buying paints for your first project, make your color selection with future stenciling projects in mind. Can two of the colors from one project be mixed to produce shades for the next project? Remember that those little cans contain enough paint to stencil the walls of several homes. And your collection will soon grow from two or three cans or jars of paint to a dozen or more as you move from one stenciling project to another. Eventually you will have enough colors to produce virtually any color combination you can imagine.

❦ 4 ❧

Color & Design

❦ WELL-KNOWN FACT of interior design is that nothing provides more instant decorating mileage than fresh paint and new fabrics. Both are fairly inexpensive ways to add color and design to a room because both are capable of covering a lot of space. A living room with sofa, chairs, tables, and accessories that have little in common but their age and condition can be brought together visually when walls, curtains, and upholstery are redone in complementary colors and patterns.

Stenciling can produce the same kind of decorative transformation at a fraction of the cost of repainting, reupholstering, or redraping. Dull walls and drab curtains in a dining room can take on new and interesting life when they are stenciled in matching floral or geometric borders of the same colors or different colors. They now have something in common: color and design. If a smaller version of one stencil, or a portion of the same stencil, is then repeated on a tablecloth, place mats, and napkins, the room begins to take on a definite personality, especially if the stenciling colors chosen were matched with one or two dominant colors already found in the room's rugs, china, lamps, pictures, furniture, or upholstery.

Stenciling Schemes

This decorative principle can be extended even further. By matching stenciling designs and colors to each room's dominant colors, you can unify the entire house. Most of us have a few favorite colors that we consciously or unconsciously plant somewhere in each room. Once these colors are narrowed down to two, three, or more, it is not hard to put them to work in an overall stenciling scheme that brings walls, curtains, bed and table linens, and furniture into decorative unity. Once you have decided on your favorite few colors, you need only choose stencil patterns that complement each other and the rooms in size and design.

If you like clean, spare lines in your rooms and furnishings, you might choose to keep your stenciling simple as well, staying with "primitives" and geometrics. Consider using a variety of uncomplicated two- or three-tone floral or geometric patterns within rooms and throughout the house. If your taste leans more toward the fancy or elaborate, you may have to work a little harder to coordinate five- or six-color Victorian florals and other intricate patterns throughout the house. Just be careful not to mix it up too much in one room, or use too many different color combinations throughout the house, or you may end up with a case of "stenciling overload." In most cases, the key to stenciling unity is simplicity, a key that you will want to keep uppermost in mind, should you decide to stencil several different kinds of surfaces and objects within one room.

Simplicity

In this book, simplicity is *the key* to successful stenciling. Simplicity is especially important for a beginner. You may not be prepared for the consequences of tackling something like a foot-high, five-color, Victorian-style border, for instance. First the border—an elaborate floral, naturally—is apt to be much too wide for anything but a ballroom, giving the walls of a normal-size room a distinctively top-heavy look. Now a complementary border is needed at the base of the walls to help balance the floral banner at the top. But this border must be narrower, otherwise the room would look gift-wrapped. Then the stenciler would need to decide whether to use all five colors in the narrow border, which would be unlikely, or just one or two of them.

Which colors should you use? Before deciding, ask yourself if the five colors at the ceiling go together, really, or whether they look more like coordinated confetti. Finally, determine whether either of the borders should be repeated around the windows and doors, or whether that would be overwhelming. (I would hope the stenciler suspects so before this point, but it's surprising how often someone will stencil first and ask these questions later.)

For many tastes, a simple one- or two-color border in a plain, open pattern is enough to brighten
the edge of a window or the tops of walls. A
complicated or multicolored stencil pattern may
produce "stenciling overkill," especially if the
stenciling is used on many surfaces within one
room.

What about the adjoining room? Should the same pattern, a portion of the pattern, or a different pattern altogether be used in there? *Is* there another stencil pattern in the world that will complement the one that has just been lavished on the first room? It gets more and more complicated until our erstwhile stenciler decides to take up stained glass making instead.

Added to the design and color problems of working with intricate stencils like the one described above are problems of simple execution. The stenciler needs five brushes, five paint containers (and woe to her is she is working with japan paint), five stencil plates, and for all I know, five arms if she plans to have the room finished sometime during that same season. You see my point, despite the hyperbole: it is far better to start off simple and get complicated later on, *after* you have developed a feel for the right designs and colors for your rooms. By using fewer colors—no more than three per stencil pattern—you will reduce your chances of choosing paint colors that clash with each other, with colors already found in the room, or with colors in other rooms.

The same holds true for stencil patterns. Simple patterns are easier to work with, especially in a border stencil, because they are easier to shade and to fit into tight places. They are less apt to tear than stencils with tiny openings, and if they do tear they are easier to patch. But most important, a simple pattern will give you much more stenciling mileage. It can be used more often and over a greater amount of space. You will also find that matching shapes and colors found in one room to stencil patterns and colors in other rooms is much easier. In addition, simple stencil patterns tend to age much better than elaborate ones. If you stencil your dining room in the ornate style described a little earlier, you may find yourself eating in the kitchen after a couple of years.

Spots or Borders?

Who can resist tackling a large, elaborate, multicolored bouquet of flowers? Large spot stencils *do* have their place. They allow you to give sway to the urge to create large, lavish stenciling without overwhelming a room. Large spot stencils are usually much more intricate than border stencils, but they can afford to be when they are used in moderation and in isolation. Large spot stencils are used to best effect in places with plenty of blank space left around them. They work well on the vertical wall spaces created by two adjoining windows or doors, above or below wainscoting, up a stairwell following the angle of the stairs, and in other spaces and places that form an ample vertical or horizontal "frame" for them.

Large, yet simple, two- or three-color spots are used most effectively on isolated surfaces, such as stair risers, with a generous amount of background surface showing around them. The stencils here do a lot of decorative work with the least amount of fuss.

With large, multicolored spot stencils you must learn to trust your tastes. I personally do not care for closely spaced columns of large spots marching in unison around a room, especially a small one, for the same reason that I don't care for stenciling that covers an entire wall. To my eye, the effect is claustrophobic and monotonous. But when used in moderation, large spot stencils can have quite an impact on bare, forlorn areas, and on furniture and other objects that have little inherent beauty because of an uninspiring design or because of the materials from which they are made.

Naturally, if you fall in love with a large spot stencil and want to cover a wall with it, go ahead. But remember, color as much as pattern can determine whether stenciling dominates a room too much. If you must have columns of foot-high pineapples or birds on your walls, consider keeping the colors muted. In fact, this is a good principle to keep in mind for all spot stencils, whether they are used often or sparingly. The appeal of bright reds, blues, greens, and yellows is sure to fade quicker than more subtle shades of rose, lavender, and sage. And should the room's furnishings change over time, the last three colors have a far better chance of living with the new items in peaceful coexistence.

Scale

Try to keep scale in mind when choosing your stencil patterns. Small or cluttered areas such as kitchens, dens, and bathrooms should be stenciled in narrow, simple borders—especially if you want to stencil around cabinets, windows, doors, and other openings and projections. Large, open rooms such as dining rooms, living rooms, and bedrooms can better accommodate larger and more colorful stenciling patterns. But simple florals and geometrics in no more than two or three colors are easier to match in adjoining rooms and prevent visual congestion.

If your taste in color and design is conservative, use very narrow borders at baseboards and around wall openings. Use the narrow portion of a larger border stencil for this purpose, or use a narrow border only at the top and bottom of a room. If you don't like surprises—if, like me, you'd prefer to change the shape of things gradually—omit the baseboard stenciling altogether at first until you have made up your mind about the ceiling stenciling. Or consider stenciling only one plate and one color at a time, at the ceiling, say, to see how you like that before adding the rest of the pattern and colors. You might decide, as I did the first time I stenciled a room, that a portion of a pattern in one color is sufficient. This is especially true if you are having a tough time finding the right colors. It's easier to find *one* color that you're sure of, use it,

Your own eye is the best aesthetic judge when combining complementary stenciling patterns. Here are three different-yet-compatible spot stencils that could work together in the same room because each is simple in style, similar in size and appearance, and limited to no more than two colors each.

then add subsequent color later on, when you know what color combination will work best in the room.

When choosing a stencil pattern for a room, try to visualize its final effect before using it. How will border stenciling look when paired later on with large spot stencils on furniture or fabrics? Will you match the colors in the two patterns or choose different but complementary colors for each? If you'd like different stenciling in the next room, will you use all or part of the pattern in the first room? Will you use the same colors, or different colors? Do you plan to change the room's furnishings or to repaint the walls in the near future? If so, you'll want to keep those new colors in mind. The more you manage to narrow down your taste in color and design *before* shopping for stenciling supplies, the easier (and cheaper) it will be to make the right choices when you find yourself confronted with a shop full of possibilities.

Planning Ahead

You do not want to begin thinking about stenciling schemes in the stencil shop. Otherwise, you will be overwhelmed by the variety of paints, stencil patterns, and other supplies that a well-stocked stencil shop has to offer. Once you multiply the stenciling possibilities in one room by the number of rooms in your home, the projects can seem positively daunting, unless you take the time to hone your stenciling plans beforehand. Have a fair idea of the *style* of stenciling you like, the colors you want, and the brushes and other supplies you'll need before you go shopping.

Where should you begin stenciling? Projects are nearly endless, but some good starting places are stairwells and foyers (the two places most often needing some kind of visual relief), stair risers (one of the easiest places to measure and stencil with spots, which never fail to impress visitors), halls, walls, ceilings, and baseboards, the perimeters of floors, doors, and windows, linens (curtains, tablecloths, napkins, place mats, clothing, bedspreads), furniture (chests, dressers, tables, chairs), small pieces (mirror frames, baskets, pegboards, boxes, plaques, lapboards, shelves), tinware (pails, pitchers, trays, mugs, lamps), and paper (stationery, shopping bags, wrapping paper, gift boxes, lampshades, and desk accessories). The possibilities, as they say, are endless.

The easiest way to discover creative stenciling ideas is to swipe them. Look around for stenciling that you admire. Visit stores and shops that sell both stenciling supplies and finished stenciled pieces. Many furniture stores now sell stenciled furniture. Look for stenciled walls and floors, curtains and furniture in decorating magazines and note how several patterns and colors have been combined in one room. You will be surprised how quickly you develop your own preferences for color and design and how they begin to assert themselves. Soon you'll be able to visualize how a stencil pattern in one color scheme might look on a piece of furniture, a wall, or a pair of curtains produced in the color scheme that, so far, is still in your mind.

❧ 5 ❧

Stenciling
Walls

ONE GOOD AND USEFUL stenciling book asserts that preparing a wall for stenciling is simple. Just wash it thoroughly, sand it, and repaint it. I assume the other walls in the room should also be washed, sanded and repainted. Then the author (and, to be fair, the authors of other stenciling books) instructs the reader to draw each room "to scale" on paper, measure the wall space and pattern sizes on the paper, then transfer corresponding chalklines for the stenciling onto the walls. Uh-huh. And while I'm at it, I'll just pick up some lumber and build a gazebo while the walls are drying.

It is not that I don't appreciate the pro's dedication to care and precision—to doing a job *right*. It's just that I'd prefer not to spend my time (not to mention my brainpower) planning and executing a stenciling project with the determination of an engineer building a four-lane bridge. I assume most beginning stencilers would not care to, either. Chalklines and graph paper are two more reasons why I prefer not to do *overall* wall and floor stenciling (what's wrong with wallpaper and rugs?), or three or more stencil patterns on the walls of one room. It just gets too darned *complicated*. All of that transferring, measuring, and marking for large, elaborate stenciling just begs the beginner and busy-but-hopeful experienced stenciler to mess up. Or to give up before she's even learned how to scale a room down to 8-by-11-inch graph paper.

Besides, if a major aim of stenciling is to add some decorative drama for little time and expense, much of what the pros would have us do in the way of "prep work" would seem to contradict both goals. Why not go the simpler route and let the stenciling materials work for us? Let's assume, first, that if you are living happily with-in four walls, then the color and condition of those walls is proba-bly okay. They don't need to be freshened with a couple of coats of paint, or even washed. If you plan to paint them anyway, then by all means do so before you stencil them. But if they are fine as they are, japan paint will adhere to them. If it doesn't, for some reason, then lightly dust, wash, or sand the area to be stenciled—not the whole wall—and the paint will cling like bats in a belfry.

Preparing Walls

To get your walls ready for stenciling, all you need to do is to dust or vacuum them for dust, cobwebs, and other debris that you never notice until you have an occasion to look upwards. Clean wherev-er the border (or spot) stenciling will go—at ceiling and baseboard, around windows and doors. If they need it badly, you should prob-ably wipe down the entire surface of the walls. But if they are presentable enough as they are, then they're ready for the brush. If you like, you can sand the surface lightly for better paint coverage and adherence, but this isn't necessary unless the walls are very glossy. Whatever you do, don't assume that the walls are dust-free where your stenciling will go. At the very least you should run the brush attachment of your vacuum at ceilings and baseboards, paying close attention to the tops of doors and windows where dust settles quietly into little shelves of dirt. There is nothing more irritating than picking up a brush-full of last summer's road dust.

Stenciling Borders

In most cases, and with most border designs, you can use the edge of your stencil plate as a guide when stenciling around ceilings, doors, windows, and baseboards. The 2- or 3-inch space at either side of the pattern will usually provide the right amount of space—aesthetically speaking—between stenciling and ceiling, baseboard, doors, and windows. The only time it might not work is when the tops of doors and windows are too close to the ceiling. To avoid the discovery of this unhappy fact in the middle of your stenciling, simply give the areas to be stenciled a quick visual pre-view. Before stenciling, take a look at the route your stenciling will travel. Place one of the stencil plates above and to the sides of all windows, doors, and other openings to make sure it has enough clearance. If it doesn't, the stencil will have to be bent or trimmed to fit, but you should know this in advance, not after you've already stenciled the entire wall that precedes the window.

The vertical and horizontal edges of doors, windows, and walls provide natural placement guides for border stencils. When the edge of the stencil plate is held flush against the edge of one of these surfaces, the stenciling comes out evenly all the way around.

Using the stencil plate as a guide, fit it into corners and other tight places to see how it will work. Are there any other obstructions along your route? Refrigerator? Cabinets? Trap door in the ceiling? If so, how will you manage them? Will you work the stenciling around them, or ignore them altogether? If you look for all of these "breaks" in your border before you begin, you can probably solve any tactical problems that might arise before you start stenciling.

If you are working with large, elaborate borders or big spot stencils, you'll have to use a little more forethought. If you plan to use a large border in a tight vertical space or a horizontal space, place the stencil plate on the surface of the wall where it will go and see how many times it will fit in there. Decide where you want to start the stencil to avoid ending the border on a partial pattern, if possible. If the stencil will not fit into the space an equal number of times, and if a partial pattern at either end would look awkward, then, perhaps, the stencil pattern is too big for the space, or the space is too small for such a large pattern, or both. Maybe you should consider another pattern or settle for having a partial pattern or blank space at either end of the border to balance it all out.

The same holds true for spot stencils. Here, it might help to stencil a few pieces of blank paper and tape them onto the wall before stenciling. In fact, I would advise doing this even if you are sure they will fit. This is the best way to see how far apart a series of spot stencils should be placed. If they look too cramped or too spaced out, simply move the test stencils around until they look right.

When you've found a harmonious arrangement, lightly draw a cross on the wall where the center of each stencil will line up when it comes time to stencil them on. If you are using spots and borders together on the same wall, plan to leave enough space between both so neither looks crowded. When interspersing a border and a spot (at the ceiling, say), you should measure the length of the wall and divide it by the number of times both patterns will fit so you'll know where to start and stop the border and pick up with the spot. No eye-balling here; you will need to know exactly where each spot will go and exactly how much border stenciling will come before and after it. If you choose to use spot stencils at the corners only, then you're off the hook. No measuring will be necessary.

If you insist on using an overall pattern on your walls, or a complicated arrangement of spots and borders, get yourself a long tape measure, some chalk, and a willing partner—a mathematician, perhaps. In most cases, simple borders and sparingly used vertical or horizontal spots will not only look the best, they will also be easier to plan and stencil. A nice compromise between a simple border and an overall stenciling job is to stencil 3 or 4 feet of spot stenciling at the base of the walls below a *horizontal* border stenciling. If you're fortunate enough to have wainscotting (the horizontal molding that sometimes skirts a room approximately 3 feet up from the floor), you need only run a border stencil just above it, using the wainscotting as a guide. If your walls, like most people's, are plain, a "wainscotting" of stenciling will have a marvelous effect on them.

To measure for this horizontal border, simply use a yardstick to measure 3 feet from the floor—or however high you would like the stenciling to be—and make a chalkline around the perimeter of the room for the stenciling to follow. You may like the appearance of the finished horizontal stenciling as it is, but if you'd like a bit more stenciling impact, one that will rival overall wall stenciling, you can stencil columns of spots at 1- or 2-foot intervals below the wainscotting created by the stenciling. You can measure these columns of spots just as easily, on your own, with a yardstick and chalk, and produce a more dramatic effect than simple border stenciling without going the graph-paper route.

Now let's say you want to stencil the walls of a medium-size room–the dining room or a bedroom, for example—at ceiling and baseboard with a simple 2- or 3-color stencil pattern. After you have

Wooden wainscotting around the perimeter of a room makes an excellent counterpoint for a border stencil. Lacking wainscotting, you can duplicate the effect of one by placing a border stencil on the wall where one would be, using a yardstick and chalk draw a guide line for the stencil plates. Here, you can see how the tail end of the border stencil is picked up using register marks on the stencil plate.

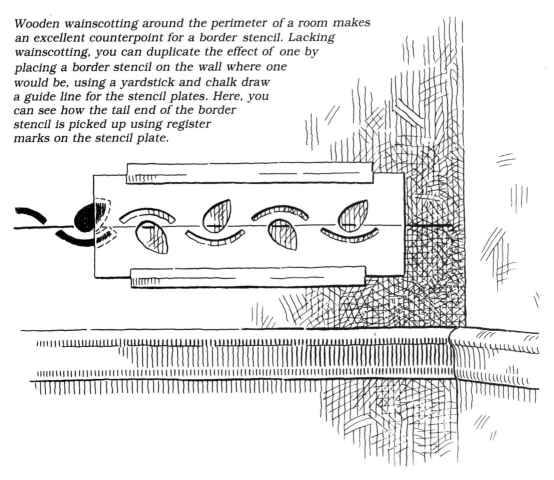

plotted out the whole route as described earlier, simply start stenciling at one corner of any wall. Using the top and left side (if you're right-handed; if you are a lefty, simply move down to the other end of the wall) of the first stencil plate as a guide, place it flush against the ceiling and the corner of the two walls. Now begin stenciling along your route, over or around doors, windows, cabinets, and other openings, until you return to the beginning of your border. It's that simple. Unless you are using a large, intricate pattern, you should have little trouble turning corners either horizontally or vertically. If you feel unsure whether you can match the stencil pattern as it turns a right angle down the side of a window or a door, read on.

Turning Corners

There are two ways in which you can make a right angle (from the horizontal to the vertical, or vice versa) turn down the side of a door, window, or other wall opening. The first is called, appropriately, a "right angle." Stencil out to the end of the horizontal (or vertical) border, then pick up the vertical (or horizontal) section *flush* with the end of the last section you stenciled—just as the letter "L" is joined together. A second way to connect horizontal and vertical borders at corners resembles the corners of a picture frame, which is called a "mitered corner". Pencil a diagonal line on the wall where the two sides of the border will meet, and place a piece of masking tape on the *bottom* side of the line. Now stencil over to the masking tape, then move the tape to the *top* of the line, and continue stenciling from that point downward. The two sides should meet perfectly at the corner.

Free-form florals and small, simple geometrics need no real planning at corners because the design, unlike that in a large, intricate border, will be easy to pick up when going in another direction. Simply turn the stencil plate around the corner and pick up the pattern at the next logical spot. "Logical," in this case, means wherever it looks "right." There's no need to make any marks on the wall or join the two sides at a right angle (the letter "L"). In fact, an open, free-form floral wouldn't look right at all if it were joined this way—it should flow around the corner as though it "grew" that way. A final note: unless you are stenciling a very small room with a large border design, all of the room's corners do not have to carry the same portion of the stencil pattern, as they would on a piece of furniture or other small object.

Stenciling a Room

Now let's get down to the actual act of stenciling. Say you've chosen a simple and narrow (1 to 3 inches), floral or geometric border for your kitchen. You have decided on your color or colors, dusted or vacuumed the walls, figured out your stenciling route, and have taken the time to measure with chalk and yardstick where you will stencil any spots or columns of spots. Begin by assembling *all* of your supplies on a large, empty (protected) table: japan paints (unless the wall is very dull and can take a water-based textile paint), turpentine for thinning the japan paint, a brush for each color, your stencil plates (cut out, of course, if necessary), mineral spirits for cleaning your brushes afterward and cleaning off any mistakes, paper towels for blotting excess paint off the brush and for cleaning up, blank paper for practicing and making "proofs" for spots and borders, masking tape to hold the stencil plates and proofs in place on the wall, and a cookie sheet or other flat spacious tray to hold everything in place and to move it around with you as you go.

One way to turn a corner at a window or door
is to use a spot stencil in the corner, bringing
both sides of the border stencil up to it. Another way would be to bring the two ends of the
border stenciling flush with each other like the
corner of the letter "L". Solid, geometric
borders like the one shown here must join with
some precision, while an open, free-form floral
border can be simply curved around corners.

Another way to join two ends of the same border stencil together is with a "mitered" joint using a diagonal line drawn through the corner. A strip of masking tape is placed at either side of the line and the stenciling brought up to it until the two ends of the border match perfectly.

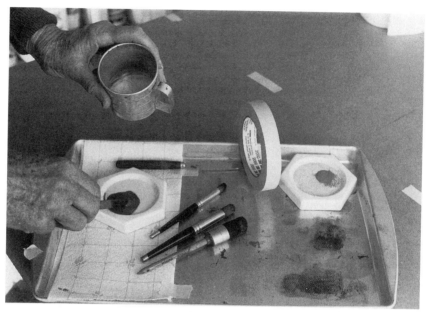

Wall stenciling goes so quickly that you will want all of your supplies at the ready and in one place. A cookie sheet or similar flat container allows you to carry your stenciling supplies as you move around the room.

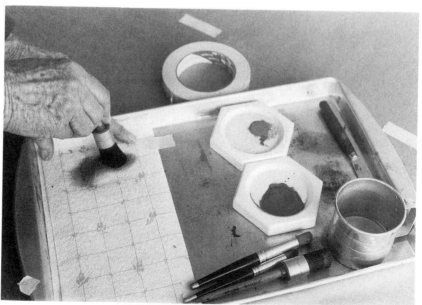

Using a well-blotted, "almost dry" brush cannot be stressed enough, especially when you are using japan paint and turpentine.

To these basic supplies, by the way, I like to add as many recyclables as I can use. Stenciling is a perfect excuse to reuse containers such as pie tins (to hold and mix the paints in), plastic coffee scoops (to mix and hold the paint), wooden ice cream sticks (to transfer paints from the cans and to mix them with turpentine), eye droppers (to add turpentine to the paint), and three plain tin cans (for cleaning brushes used with turpentine). These supplemental supplies are easy to set aside to be used later when stenciling. You will not have to hunt down containers and these disposables can be tossed out, rather than cleaned, when you have finished stenciling. If you have ever tried to remove hardened japan paint from a porcelain saucer, you will know to start saving any kind of shallow, disposable container that comes your way.

Once you have your supplies in order and a large, clear space to work from—a table, countertop, or other flat surface handy to your stenciling project—find a sturdy stool, a stepladder, or an old chair to stand on so you can reach to the top of the wall. I belong to the "get up and down" school of border stenciling, which means that I'm usually so anxious to start stenciling, rather than place my paint and paper-towel blotter nearby, I climb up on the chair or stool with nothing more than a paint-loaded brush. It will be easier if you place your pie-tin palette and paper-towel blotter on a small table or other surface near your stool, chair, or ladder so you don't have to climb down and run to the table each time you need to refill your brush. Somehow, I never get quite this organized; but if you can, it will help the job go more smoothly.

Now place a small amount of your first color for the appropriate stencil plate (probably plate 1, unless you have chosen to use only plate 2 or plate 3) on a pie tin or other shallow dish—using a wooden stick, a spoon, anything but the brush. Add a few drops of turpentine to the paint and mix it up well. Tip the very ends of the brush bristles into the paint, and blot the brush off on a folded paper towel until the brush seems dry. Now practice stenciling that first plate on paper until you get a feel for how much paint to use and at what consistency. Don't be timid about adding more paint or turpentine to the mixture until you get the right consistency (but *do* be timid about how much paint you put on the brush). Take a little time with this exercise, because what you finally see stenciled on the paper is pretty much what it will look like on your walls. Keep practicing until you feel confident that you can produce a clear, sharp impression with the stencil, without moving the plate or smearing the paint.

Work on your shading. If the brush gets gunky, add a little turpentine to the paint. If the paint seems too liquidy, add more paint until it seems thick enough. When you think you've got it all mastered, get up on the stool with your plate and brush, and start stenciling.

At first, it will help to tape a 2- or 3-inch piece of masking tape to the bottom edge of the stencil plate to help you keep it in place on the wall. After a few feet of the border is stenciled on, however, you'll probably find that you can hold the stencil firmly and evenly without help from the masking tape. Be sure to hold the plate still and flat against the wall, with your fingers pressing down on the outlines of the pattern as you brush the paint on.

Apply the paint as you did on your successful paper proofs. Give the paint a moment or two to dry, then lift the plate straight out from the wall, taking care not to shift it, or the paint will smudge. Does the stencil look clear, sharp and well shaded? Are you happy with it? If not, immediately wipe it off with a little turpentine or, if you're using textile paint, with a damp cloth and a little soap. If you've taken the time to practice on paper, your very first impression should be clean. If not, wipe it off and redo it, or you'll notice it a hundred times a year after the entire room is stenciled.

Move the stencil plate to the right, using the register marks to pick up the tail end of the pattern you just stenciled on. Thin and

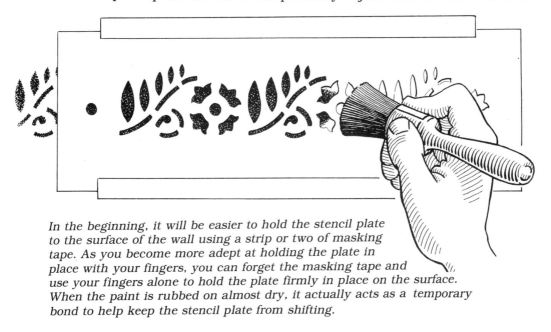

In the beginning, it will be easier to hold the stencil plate to the surface of the wall using a strip or two of masking tape. As you become more adept at holding the plate in place with your fingers, you can forget the masking tape and use your fingers alone to hold the plate firmly in place on the surface. When the paint is rubbed on almost dry, it actually acts as a temporary bond to help keep the stencil plate from shifting.

replenish your paint when necessary, taking care to blot the brush well before stenciling. Should you have to leave the scene for an hour or so, you can avoid cleaning the brush by wrapping it in plastic wrap until you return. When you reach your first corner, carefully bend the stencil all the way into it, hold it firmly, and paint in as much of the pattern as you can before picking it up again on the next wall. When you reach a cabinet, window, or other framable ''interruption'' in the wall, do as you had planned before stenciling—either continue to stencil above the window, door, or whatever, or turn your stencil and go around it.

Remember to keep your paint at the right consistency at all times and to hold the edges of the stencil pattern firmly beneath your fingers, applying the paint in circular, shading motions. Do not worry if the paint coverage or shading varies somewhat from impression to impression—as I said earlier, this is what gives stenciling its handcrafted appearance. You will find your first stenciling job going quickly and easily, and you'll be pleasantly surprised by your ability to produce beautiful, clear, well-shaded impressions on your first try.

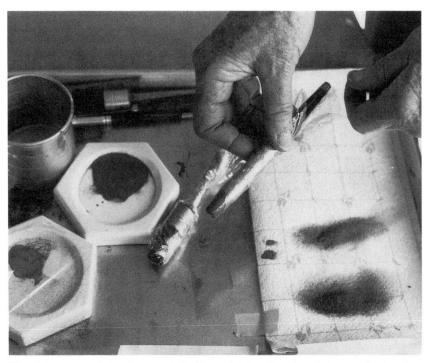

Should you need to stop work in the middle of a stenciling project using japan paint, you can keep the paint-filled brush from drying out by wrapping it in clear plastic.

When you reach a corner with the border stencil, bend the plate into the corner as far as you can and stencil in as much of the pattern as you can reach. Then simply pick the next portion of the pattern up on the other wall, and continue stenciling. Masking tape may help to hold the plate in the corner until it is stenciled in on either side.

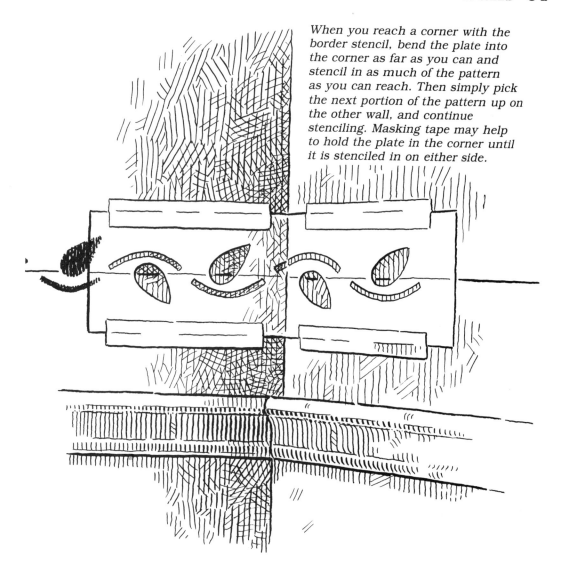

Cleanup

After you have stenciled the entire border at the tops of the walls, step back and take a look at it. Is that one color enough for the room right now? You may decide that it is for the time being. If not, do you have enough time today to add the second and third paint colors? Remember that you have to factor in some cleaning time, allowing for each time you use a new plate and paint color, so it may be better to continue stenciling another day. Either way, give yourself a breather by cleaning the brush and stencil plate you just used. If you put this off until later, you'll probably be sorry you did.

The second plate of the pattern is being stenciled on top of the first plate of this three-color border stencil. In the beginning, masking tape will help keep the stencil plate flush with the wall to prevent paint from seeping past the edges of the pattern.

Remember, the paint dries as quickly on the brush and plate, as it dries on your walls.

If you have used textile paint, cleanup will be a breeze. Simply wash the brush well with soap and water, dry it off, and stick it somewhere so the bristles can air-dry pointed upwards. Wash the stencil plate off with soap and water, being careful not to scrub so hard that you stretch or tear the pattern: then dry it, and put it aside. Tear off a few fresh paper towels, and you're ready to go on with your stenciling.

If you are using japan paint, first close the can of the first color *tightly* and store it upside down to keep the pigment near the top of the can. Pour a small amount of mineral spirits into each of three tin cans, and give the used brush a quick rinse in each until it comes out clean. Rub the bristles dry with a clean paper towel or rag, then wash the brush well in soap and water to remove oily film left by the mineral spirits. Leave the brush out to air-dry. If the brush is a large one, you might want to place a rubber band around the bristles to keep them together.

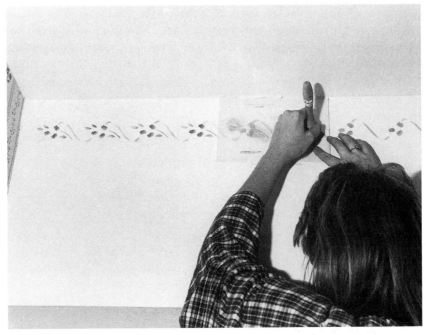

Plate three, and the third color, is now stenciled on top of plates 1 and 2. Although the stenciling is turning out well—finely shaded, with crisp, clean outlines—this "lefty" should probably be working from right-to-left instead of left-to-right.

Now tackle the stencil plate with the mineral spirits as well, using a very soft brush, old sponge, or rag to get all of the paint off, especially around the edges of the pattern, where it accumulates the most. If you don't clean japan paint from your stencil plate as soon as possible, turpentine will react with the old paint the next time you use it, and if you are using a different color, you may find yourself "custom mixing" two colors right on the wall. When all of the paint is off, wash the stencil plate with soap and water and wipe it dry. Clean off the pie tin and other containers and implements for later use, or toss them out. Save your best practice stencils of the first plate and toss out all used paper towels so the first paint doesn't accidentally get on your clean plates and brushes. Now practice with plate 2 on top of plate 1. Once you see how to align the two to your satisfaction, stencil on the second color on top of the first.

The finished stenciling will need no protection. After 6 months or so, you can wash it down with mild soap and water and it won't smear, flake, or rub off the wall.

A final word about border stenciling versus overall stenciling. When the time does come to repaint the walls, it will be much easier to sand down a narrow band or two of stenciling, or a few spot stencils, so the new paint covers them well. You can imagine how difficult it might be to paint over four walls' worth of pineapples —ask any house painter.

Japan paint must be cleaned off brushes thoroughly before the brushes can be used again, otherwise paint residues may become mixed with a fresh color. The best way to clean brushes used with japan paint is to add a little mineral spirits to each of three cans and rinse the brush out in each can until, on the third rinse, it comes out clean. Wash it well with soap and water, dry it off, and allow it to air dry with the bristles pointed upward.

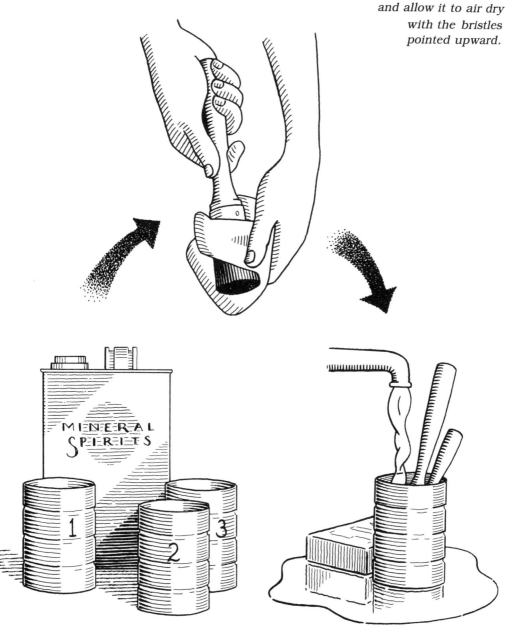

Stencil plates— especially those used with japan paint—should be cleaned immediately after use. Use turpentine or mineral spirits to clean off japan paint or soap and water to clean off textile paint. Clean the paint off with a paper towel, rag, or soft brush, taking care not to tear or stretch the contours of the stencil pattern. Rinse the plate in clear water, blot it dry, and it will be good as new for future use. If the stencil paint is allowed to dry on the plate, it will be difficult, if not impossible, to remove later.

❧ 6 ❧

Stenciling Floors

BY NOW YOU MAY have figured out that to stencil a floor, you need only readjust your perspective from the vertical to the horizontal. Or, from standing on a stool to sitting down. Stenciling a floor border, after all, means working with the same kind of square or rectangular perimeter that you find at the tops and bottoms of walls. In fact, floor stenciling can be easier because you will encounter fewer obstacles such as doors, windows, and cabinets, and you can sit—or even lie down—while you work, rather than kneel or balance yourself precariously on a stool or chair.

As long as a wood floor has a reasonably undamaged stained or painted finish, it will take japan paint, although it is a good idea to remove any heavy buildup of wax with mineral spirits and soap and water before stenciling. To give the stenciling the best chance of adhering, rub the border area down lightly with fine steel wool or extra-fine sandpaper before stenciling.

An overall stenciling job can be stunning, but again, as with overall stenciling on walls, I have a long list of reasons for not recommending it to beginners. My top three objections are time, work, and expense. The floor must first be stripped, because an overall stenciling design in a large room requires *much* better adherence than a border design will. Consider the amount of traffic that any room receives over a period of time and you'll see what I mean. In addition, if the stenciling is to have some visual impact over the wood, it must remain vivid.

After stripping off all of the old varnish and wax, the floor must be sanded, and this involves the time and expense I just mentioned.

Unless you have one and are handy with a machine sander, you must call in a pro (at great expense) or actually hand-sand the floor yourself (too much time—not to mention muscle). The floor must then be stained or painted, depending on your preference, with at least two coats of either. Naturally, all of the room's furniture must be taken out before any of this begins, and the room itself will be out of commission for a good week or so by the time the floor is properly prepared, measured out (the graph paper again), stenciled, then sealed with two or three coats of varnish to protect the stenciling.

It is daunting work, it can't be skimped on, and as you can imagine, placement of the stenciling is critical. A minor error in measurement on the graph paper or the chalklines that are used to lay out the stenciling on the floor will grow into a monumental one when the stenciling is transferred onto a 12-by-12-foot floor. You will do far better to start out with a nice, clean border stenciling or stenciled floor cloth (which I'll describe later on in this chapter for those who want some central floor stenciling and for whose who do not have wooden floors) and save an overall floor-stenciling project for later, when you have either the funds or the nerve to try it.

Border Stenciling

I have stenciled with japan paint on normally finished wood floors (stained, varnished, and lightly waxed) and can attest that the paint does adhere. The stenciling is there to prove it. For one thing, it is still there because a border stencil does not receive anywhere near the amount of wear that an overall stencil pattern does from hard-soled shoes, scraping chair legs, and romping pets and children. Much of a border stencil is protected by its very position—away from normal, everyday traffic and under furniture.

A couple of coats of low-gloss varnish or good paste wax will give it further protection. Exposed sections of a wide border across a doorway or other opening into a room can be touched up easily if scuffed. And if you use an open, free-form floral or geometric border instead of a wide, enclosed banner, the wear will be even less noticeable and even easier to repair.

Doorway problems are eliminated altogether if you stencil on a narrow, free-form pattern because the stenciling will stop at either side of the door. A wide, solid border would look odd unless it continued around the whole room, including the space in front of a doorway.

Color and Design

Color for floor stenciling is a matter of taste. Depending on the color of the floor, the style of the room, and the colors of its furnishings, you may choose a pastel color combination or a pattern of deep, rich colors. If the stencil pattern is fine and delicate and the floor is dark, you may choose to use light colors applied heavily, or dark colors applied lightly. On a dark floor, light or medium shades might disappear into the floor or wear out too quickly. For this reason, you might want to apply more paint and use less shading than you would on wall stenciling.

If you are unsure about the right design, colors, and density of paint, fall back on your paper proofs, even going so far as to cut the pattern out of the paper and place it directly onto the floor to see how it looks. Of course, paint will look different once it is applied to the wood floor. To see how all of this will come together on the floor, have a rag and turpentine ready, and try it out right on the floor. Don't be afraid to test stencil japan paints and patterns out this way on walls and other hard, shiny surfaces. So long as you can wipe the paint off before it dries, without leaving any traces of it on the surface, you won't ruin anything and you will be able to stencil right over it.

If, for some reason, you can't get all of the japan paint off of the floor after testing a paint color or pattern, rub the spot lightly with steel wool or sandpaper. So long as you don't make the border area of the floor much lighter or less glossy than the rest of the floor by wiping, cleaning, and sanding too much, you can experiment with colors and designs until you're happy with the results. Just don't try test stenciling with japan paint or textile paint on fabrics or other dull, porous surfaces. Once either type of paint is applied to these, it is usually there to stay.

Remember, your stencil pattern, the size of the pattern, and the colors you use will also depend on any stenciling you have applied to the walls around the floor. If you have used a great deal of stenciling on the walls—ceiling and baseboard borders, borders around windows and doors, and spot stenciling—you will have to be judicious about the colors and pattern, if any, you use on the floor. You don't want to mix things up so much that you experience vertigo whenever you walk into the room.

Preparing the Floor

To ready a floor for a border stencil, pull the furniture away from the walls, vacuum the border area thoroughly, and then wash it. If the wax looks heavy or if the varnish is thick, wipe the area down with mineral spirits, then clean that off with soap and water, and rub the floor down with fine steel wool or extra-fine sandpaper until the paint adheres. Rub it lightly and quickly; there's no need to spend all day sanding. And you want to be careful that the depth and shine of the border finish approximates the finish on the rest of the floor. If, on the other hand, you are using wide, solid border stenciling, you can take the finish down as much as you desire, because the stenciling will obscure any discrepancies between that area and the rest of the floor. In fact, if you have a very dark, heavily varnished floor, you may have to use a solid border stencil in order to make the stenciling adhere to the surface of the floor.

Stenciling the Floor Border

Once you've moved the furniture, prepared the floor, and gathered all the usual supplies, position yourself at the *center* of one of the walls; it doesn't matter which wall. If you start stenciling out from the center of each wall, the borders will match up perfectly on all sides, an important consideration when you are using a wide border with large patterns. Otherwise, the stenciling will look unbalanced and will not match up at all four corners.

If the border is a curvy floral, you will have a little more latitude, but it is still a good idea to begin stenciling from the center of each wall outward, unless the pattern is a narrow one for a small room. In that case, it won't matter whether the patterns stenciled at the four corners match.

Stencil up to about 6 inches from each corner, leaving the corners for last. Then stencil in each of the four corners, handling them as you would when stenciling around a door or a window. If the border is a curving floral, simply curve it around each corner. If it is a wide, enclosed banner of flowers or geometrics, have the corners meet at right angles or joined like the corners of a picture frame, as described in the last chapter. Once you have stenciled the entire border in using all of the colors in the pattern, allow the stenciling to dry for *at least* 24 hours, then give it two or three coats of varnish or hard paste wax. Be sure to rub each coat of varnish down with fine steel wool or sandpaper before adding the next to give each coat a chance to adhere and to avoid an overly glossy or thick finish over the stenciling. The varnish or paste wax will protect the stenciling against normal wear and tear and will bring out the colors of the japan paint as well.

If the finished border looks too shiny for the rest of the floor, dull it a little with steel wool and rewax it. Keep everything—dust, children, and pets—away from the varnish until it has dried thoroughly (at least 24 hours for each coat), then move the furniture back into place. Your stenciling should be durable, long-lasting, and beautiful to behold.

If you want to get rid of your border stencil for some reason after a year or so, get yourself a can of the varnish remover that antiques dealers use to remove the *varnish only* from furniture. A good brand

A simple, yet very effective, floor border combines a simple geometric and abstract floral at corners. Such borders are easy to stencil and to protect, and if part of the pattern becomes worn after use, it will be easy to touch up.

is Parks Furniture Refinisher. This refinisher is not the pasty kind that is used to scrap off old paint and varnish. It looks and smells like alcohol, instead. Rub it on the stenciling, sparingly, with steel wool until the stenciling comes off, then varnish, wax, and buff the area until it looks like the rest of the floor. Incidentally, Parks Furniture Refinisher is an excellent product for cleaning up the old pieces of wood furniture you will find at auctions, flea markets, and other places in order to ready them for the stenciling described in a later chapter. I recommend it highly.

Spot Stenciling a Small Floor

Now, let's say that you want some large spot stencils somewhere under foot. A border stencil isn't enough for the room you have in mind. Short of stenciling the entire floor, and preparing it as described earlier, you have a couple of choices. You can try an overall design on a small floor—in a bathroom, kitchenette, or small study, if you like. Here, the prep work for stripping, sanding, staining, or painting can be managed by hand without undue stress. I didn't mention this earlier in the heat of the discussion about overall stenciling on large floors because it would have diluted my argument. Naturally, any space can be stenciled, no matter how large or small, depending upon the stenciler's industry and purse. But in a book for beginners, small and simple really is better.

Stripping and Sanding

To stencil a small floor, first make sure you can keep everything and everyone out of the room for a few days to give yourself enough time to prepare, stencil, and finish it. If the floor is painted or has a heavy finish of varnish, you will first have to strip it with paint remover—the thick, pasty kind meant to remove paint as well as varnish. You will then have to sand it smooth by hand or with a small hand-sander, and then restain it, unless you like the the way the floor appears after sanding.

Materials for stripping are as follows: 2 or 3 quarts of paint remover (Red Devil is a good brand); a scraper to remove the varnish or other finish lifted off by the remover; several coffee cans to receive the gunk you scrape off; good, thick rubber gloves to protect your hands; and a small paper face mask (available at all hardware stores) to protect yourself from the fumes. This is not as messy or toxic as it sounds. As long as the room is fairly well ventilated, and as long as you keep those gloves and mask on, the work won't be that odious. Just be careful not to get the remover on your skin, and be sure to have plenty of containers on hand to receive the old finish as you scrape it up.

Once all of the old finish has been removed, take a couple of old sheets and drape them over anything you wouldn't want to get sawdust on. Have *plenty* of fine sandpaper on hand, and sand the floor in the direction of the grain until it is smooth and all traces of the old finish have vanished. The better your sanding job, the nicer the floor and stenciling will look afterwards.

When the floor is sanded, vacuum it thoroughly to remove absolutely all dust. Now stain the floor with any color stain you like, keeping your stenciling colors in mind. Let it dry overnight, and it should be ready for stenciling the next day. If the weather is humid or cold, it may take a little longer for the stain to dry. And if the first coat of stain is not dark enough, you will have to give it another coat—and let that dry—before stenciling the floor.

Measuring for Stenciling

To measure the floor for spot stenciling, take a yardstick and piece of chalk, draw vertical and horizontal lines until the entire floor is covered in squares. Prepare some paper stencils, and place those stencils—cut out of the paper, if you really want to see how they will look before stenciling the pattern—either on every intersection of the chalk lines or every other intersection. See which arrangement you like best. If you want a free-form arrangement, cut out enough stencils to cover the entire floor, then move them around until you find a pleasing arrangement. Mark the spot where each will go, and you're ready to stencil on the design.

If you want a border around your spot stencils, stencil that on before you draw your grid of squares. Stenciled or solid borders can be marked off with masking tape, which can also be used as a guide to align a border stencil or a solid border of paint. Any errors in measurement on a small floor will be evident *before* you begin stenciling, and maintenance will be minimal because you'll have a smaller space to protect. When the stenciling has dried for 24 hours, protect it with two coats of varnish, rubbed down with fine steel wool between coats, and finish it off with a coat of paste wax.

Canvas Floor Cloths

Stenciled floor cloths have certain advantages over stenciled floors. You don't have to worry so much about color and design permanently altering the character of a room. A floor cloth can be moved out of the way of heavy traffic, or out of a room altogether. And a floor cloth can be stenciled to any size. Heavy No. 8 or No. 10 canvas is used for these floor coverings. The canvas comes in roll widths of 3, 4, 5, 6, and 10 feet, and can be purchased from a canvas supplier if there is one near you. If not, refer to the appendix of this book for more information.

Most floor cloths look best when stenciled with a solid border surrounding central spot stenciling, with a generous amount of the contrasting background showing around the spots. A contrasting light or dark background will make the stenciling stand out vividly. One of the easiest and best-looking floor cloth designs has a white or natural background bordered in solid dark red, blue, or green paint. Large (6- to 8-inch) spots are stenciled inside the border. The

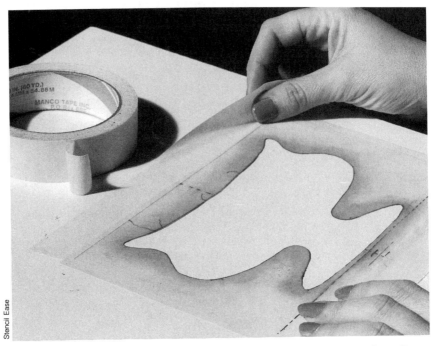

Stencil Ease

Very large spot stencils must be taped down securely to keep them from shifting when the paint is applied.

spots consist of no more than two colors (red and green, for example), one of which matches the solid border. This simple scheme will allow you to stencil without worrying that any of the colors will run together, a possibility when stenciling with japan paint on cloth because you must apply the paint heavily enough to give the stenciling definition. A contrasting background will also give the spot stenciling definition, as will the solid border.

Stencil Patterns

The stencil patterns I have in mind for this floor cloth are reminiscent of the simple stars, tulips, hearts, and birds found in early quilts. These primitive patterns don't demand any fancy shading to give the stenciling a realistic quality, and they are simple enough to blend with a great many decors—a consideration if you plan to move the floor cloth into different rooms for a change of pace.

The spots can be arranged in any way you like. Try finding a pleasing arrangement by using paper proofs. The easiest and most effective arrangement consists of a large central spot flanked on either side by two slightly smaller spots of a different, but complementary, pattern. You might stencil a heart, or a tulip of two colors, in the center, for example, and two birds or two stars at either side of it. With just a few different stencil patterns the possible

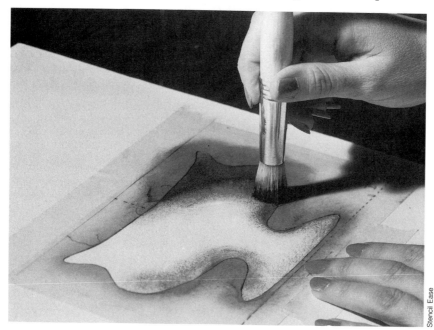

Stencil Ease

Large stencils must be shaded very gradually from the outside edges toward the center.

arrangements are nearly endless, but this five-spot arrangement is unfailingly attractive. It seems to produce the greatest impact with the fewest colors and patterns. Another advantage to using large, simple stencil patterns rather than small, intricate ones on canvas floor cloths is that, if you wish, you will have more freedom to shade them even though you will have to use more paint on this thirsty surface.

The size of the spot stenciling, the width of the border, and the amount of background space that is left to show around the stenciling will largely be a matter of your own taste. First decide how large you want the floor cloth to be. A 4-by-6-foot floor cloth is a manageable size to work with, and it will provide ample space for a 2- or 3-inch border and five 6- to 8-inch spot stencils.

Preparing the Canvas

To prepare the floor cloth for stenciling, first decide whether you want to stencil right onto the canvas. This will result in a light, neutral background and, not incidentally, require a lot less work. Or, you may want to paint the background an off-white to contrast with dark stenciling colors of blue, red, green, or other colors. If you paint the background a dark color (red, blue, green, or even black), your stenciling colors will have to be lighter by contrast. You will also need more paint to cover the dark background, and shading may be impossible. If you want to shade your stenciling, it is best to work with a neutral, unpainted floor cloth.

If you want to paint in the background, use two or three coats of semigloss latex paint, allowing each to dry completely for at least 24 hours. Because you will be using japan paint, you can paint the background any color you like, of course, and the stenciling will have good coverage. Be careful not to bend the canvas at any time. It should always be rolled, never folded. If the canvas does become creased, press it immediately with a hot iron.

Before painting or stenciling the canvas, clear out a large space on the floor and vacuum the area well. If dust or dirt falls onto the paint before it has a chance to dry, the paint will appear pebbly. You won't be able to sand it down and repaint, as you can do with wood. So take the time to clean the area well and keep activity in the room to a minimum.

You can glue or sew under the two unbound edges at either end of the floor cloth, or you can paint right over them and allow the paint to bind the loose threads together. Either method will give the rug a "finished" look on all sides, although sewing—with a heavy needle and heavy thread—will give the unfinished ends more protection. You can also turn those unfinished ends into fringe after they are painted. Give it some thought, and if you decide to sew the two unfinished ends, do it before you begin painting the background or the border.

Stenciling the Floor Cloth

Now place several thicknesses of newspaper on the floor to protect it against paint spills or smears, as well as paint seeping through the bottom of the canvas. (This is more likely to happen if you use a dark background color because you may have to use more of this paint in order to completely cover the light canvas.) Immobilize the floor cloth with thumbtacks or masking tape before applying the first coat of background color. If the canvas requires a lot of paint, it may soften and stretch out of shape. The thumbtacks or masking tape will help keep it even.

Paint the cloth evenly, using long strokes down the length of the cloth, and take care to leave as few brush strokes as possible. Take further care that the paint does not build up around the edges of the cloth or "puddle" anywhere in the center. When this coat has been applied, close the door for 24 hours until the paint has a chance to dry. Add the second coat the next day in the same manner, and again wait at least 24 hours before stenciling. When you come back with your stenciling supplies, touch the painted cloth. If it feels cool to your fingers, the paint is not quite dry. Give it some more time, or try turning the heat up in the room to help dry it out. And again, be careful not to bend the cloth, because the paint may crack.

Once the background color is thoroughly dry, or if you are working on an unpainted cloth, it's time to resume stenciling. Place the cloth on several thicknesses of clean newspaper, and hold it taut with thumbtacks or masking tape. Stenciling on virgin canvas will also require a lot of paint, some of which will also seep through the canvas. With a yardstick and chalk, measure out the solid border, and mark it off with masking tape. Make sure the tape sticks firmly so there's no chance that the stencil paint will creep beyond it and onto the center of the floor cloth. If you do this, and if you keep your paint at the right consistency (dry) you should produce a clean, even border all the way around the cloth. Now make chalk crosses where your center and side stenciling will go and use paper proofs to verify how it will all look before you begin stenciling.

Be sure to have everything assembled before you begin stenciling, particularly plenty of paint and turpentine (as well as paper towels and cleaning rags) because unpainted canvas will really soak up the paint. If you are working on a painted cloth, this will not be such a problem because the canvas has already soaked up about as much paint as it can handle. But if you are working on unpainted canvas, you'll see your stenciling almost disappear the first time you apply the paint. Just keep adding paint at the correct, dry consistency until you build up the stenciling to the right color and depth. If you try to rush it and apply too much paint at once, it will run beyond the edges of the stencil pattern, and the design will be ruined. Remember, once you stencil on cloth the paint is there to stay. On the other hand, if you are working on a painted cloth, you should be able to remove any mistakes immediately. Those are the trade-offs between painted and unpainted floor cloth backgrounds.

Because you have to use more stencil paint on canvas than you do on hard surfaces such as walls, floors, and furniture, shading may be more difficult. You need to add enough paint to give the stenciling adequate coverage and definition, yet the more paint you add, the more opaque the stenciling will turn out. There isn't much you can do about this. You'll have to decide which you like more—impact or subtlety. I would opt for the added impact that deeper color will provide, especially since the floor cloth will be underfoot and not on the walls. Also, when shading, the stencil is usually painted from the outside edges inward, to produce lighter

Stencil Ease

The border of the floor cloth can be stenciled using two parallel strips of masking tape.

color in the center of the pattern. The problem with using this shading technique on floor cloths is that as you continue to add more paint for greater coverage, you increase the risk of having the paint run beyond the edges of the pattern. On the other hand, if you decide to forego shading, you can stencil from the center of the pattern outward and use the least amount of paint on the outside edges of the stencil, reducing the risk of paint smudging or running beyond the outside edges of the pattern. That's a lot of explanation for what seems like a minor consideration; but the added emphasis is justified, when you consider the fact that it will be impossible, on an unpainted cloth, to undo any mistakes.

When stenciling, hold the plates firmly on the cloth as you would on any other surface. Use your fingers to hold the outside edges of those large patterns as flat and stable as you can. Brush the paint on slowly and carefully, keeping in mind that the goal here is not speed, but accuracy. Patiently add a little paint at a time, fiddling with the turpentine-paint mixture until the consistency seems right, and until the stencil impression suits you.

If the paint takes too long to dry as you are stenciling on more paint, remove the stencil plate—straight up, taking care not to shift it over the wet paint—and wait for the paint to dry before repositioning the stencil plate and adding more paint. You can always work on other spots while the first is drying. Be sure to keep the area and your fingers as clean of paint as possible so you don't smudge any on the background of the cloth. Double-check to see that you are using the correct side of the stencil plate, and that there is no paint clinging to the underside of it. You'd be surprised at how easy it is to make this mistake. Approach your floor cloth as you would the canvas for a painting.

Protecting the Floor Cloth

Once you've completed the stenciling to your satisfaction, allow the paint to dry for *at least* 24 hours before protecting it and the rug itself with at least two coats of varnish. If you don't let the stenciling dry, it may "bleed" below the varnish, making all of your painstaking efforts for naught. Apply the first coat of varnish—with the floor cloth placed on fresh newspaper and tacked or taped in place—in a completely dust-free area. Use a clean brush to apply the varnish in long strokes down the length of the cloth, taking care to avoid brush marks and varnish buildup at the edges.

When the first coat of varnish has dried (24 hours again), rub it down lightly with steel wool to dull it, thin it, and give the second coat some adherence. Apply the second coat as you did the first and let it dry. There is no need to rub this coat of varnish down.

If you like, you can give the floor cloth a coating of good, clear paste wax to produce a softer glow and even more protection.

Your floor cloth is now finished. It can be cleaned with mild soap and water if it becomes soiled and can be used as you would any other rug. The floor cloth will make a beautiful stenciled surface that you can walk on, place furniture on, and move from room to room. You just can't bend it, because the cloth now has several coats of paint and varnish on it that can easily crack. When moving the floor cloth around, either drag it by one end or roll it up loosely as you would a large, stiff poster.

❧ 7 ❧

Stenciling Wood

IN A PROMINENT SPOT in our bedroom sits a small, five-drawer pine chest. For a long time it was kept hidden behind closed doors, where it served as extra storage space for unused clothing and linens. My husband had the chest when he was a kid, and we thought the white paint and elephant decals would look a bit out of place among our more adult furnishings. But after we stripped the chest, stained it, and waxed it, it looked as boring as thousands of others like it. Once I discovered how easy it is to stencil furniture, however, the chest finally came out of the closet. Now it is paired with a pine mirror finished and stenciled to match, and the chest is once again honored to hold my husband's underwear and socks.

Pine

Almost any piece of furniture—and countless small wooden objects—can be transformed from standard, functional pieces of storage into minor works of decorative art. The beauty of many pieces, especially furniture, is evident in the quality and grain of their wood, and these objects need no embellishment. But many chests, bureaus, tables, mirrors, boxes, chairs, and other inexpensive "mass-produced" furniture are decidedly blah in any setting, either because of their purely utilitarian shape and function, or because they are made of uninspiring wood—often pine. As lovely as pine flooring, paneling, and some furniture is, it does tend to pale beside the richness of the grains of mahogany, walnut, oak, and other hard woods. The problem is, pine is just so *standard*. Designers don't often invest much creative effort when making pine furniture. All of the loving detail seems to be lavished on the more expensive hardwoods.

Countless small wooden objects can be stenciled in a variety of patterns. Shown here are several pantry boxes, a square box, and an oblong cassette tape holder from Pat Estey's shop, stenciled in her own designs. Note the unique stenciling style she has developed in the shading of the sheep stencil.

But a good thing about pine is that it is the perfect wood for stenciling. It is light enough in color (unless it was given a dark stain) to show off even the palest stenciling patterns. Its modest grain makes a good background for stenciling because it doesn't compete with it. Pine takes both japan and textile paints beautifully, depending upon the finish on the wood: shiny painted or varnished wood requires japan paint for adherence, while plain or stained wood can take water-based textile paint. Pine can be stenciled when plain and unfinished, stained, stained and varnished, or painted in a coat of colorful background paint.

Another benefit is that pine is usually the cheapest wood around. You can pick up unfinished or used pine pieces (unless they are antiques, of course) for a song. And if you are thinking of stenciling a piece of plain pine furniture you already own, chances are it is hidden away in a closet somewhere. So you have little to lose, right?

What to Stencil

Garage sales, yard sales, wood shops, department stores, and auctions—visit them all and you'll find plenty of good stenciling candidates. Large and small blanket chests, painted or stained, make wonderful working surfaces for stenciling. You can try your hand at stenciling large, fancy, intricate spots or mixing spots and

Water-based textile stenciling paint will adhere well to small pine objects that have been given a light-colored stain and no other finish. Only a portion of a six-color wood duck stencil plate is being used for this duck wall hanging.

borders in a way that might be too overpowering on your walls. Stool seats and tabletops are other natural "frames" within which to work when using spot stencils.

The wide backs of chairs and rockers work well as surfaces for either small spots or borders and they can be matched to coordinate with stenciling on a table. Rocking chairs usually have a nice, broad slat on the back (Boston rockers, in fact, are famous for their hand-painted or stenciled designs.) The sides of shelves and bookcases, the headboards and footboards of beds, benches, bureaus, door panels, wall paneling, mirror frames, coat racks, quilt racks, boxes, utensil trays, bookends, lamp bases, and even baskets—any and all of these surfaces, so long as they are not too curved, carved, or glossy, can be transformed with some creative stenciling.

Finished or Unfinished?

If you want to stencil an unfinished piece of pine, you can stencil directly onto it with water-based textile paint or japan paint, and varnish or paste-wax it afterwards to bring out the color of the stenciling and to give it some protection. Small pieces such as mirror frames and hanging shelves often need no stain, varnish, or wax at all. On these objects, the stenciling should remain undisturbed. But it is a simple matter to give the piece a light spraying of varnish, which will give the surface a little more gleam and make the stenciling stand out more vividly.

If you want to give a piece of pine a little more life *before* stenciling, you might give it a coat of light, clear, penetrating wood stain—not the opaque kind—before stenciling. This will bring out the subtle grain of the wood just a little and still keep the wood in the background of the stenciling. I like to use light-colored, penetrating wood stains by Minwax: Fruitwood, Puritan Pine, Driftwood, and Natural all produce nice, light background stains for stenciling. This company also manufactures an excellent clear

Small wooden objects such as this pine mirror frame make it easy to experiment with different spots and borders. The straight, narrow edges produce an easy guide for the border stenciling and the rise at the top makes a natural "frame" for the spot stenciling. Because this mirror will not receive much handling, it is possible to stencil it with textile paint, either over bare wood or over a light-colored stain. And it would require no varnish or other protective finish over the stenciling.

A similar pine wall-hanging stenciled in the same brown-and-green paint combination shown in the photos on pages 73 and 76. This piece was sprayed lightly with varnish once the stenciling had dried thoroughly. While varnish is not necessary to protect small pieces that will not receive any wear, it does help to bring out the colors in the stenciling.

Large pieces of furniture such as this pine blanket chest benefit from a hard, oil-based background paint for extra protection. Japan paint is used for vivid color, adherence, and durability. A coat or two of varnish is needed to protect the finished stenciling.

paste wax for finishing, and its refinishing products are also exceptionally good. Keep in mind that you may have to remove old paint and varnish from old pieces—even if you plan to paint them before stenciling them. You will want a *smooth* surface for your stenciling, not one that is bumpy with aged varnish or paint.

One drawback to stenciling directly onto bare pine is that, as with stenciling fabric and floor cloths, there are no second chances, whether you are using japan paint or textile paint. The stenciling can't be wiped off, reapplied, or "corrected" if you mess up or use the wrong colors. A safeguard against this possibility is to spray the piece lightly with varnish. This way, if you position the stencil plate wrong or smudge or smear the paint, you'll be able to wipe the stencil off before it dries. But if you practice first on paper, keep your brush dry, and hold the stencil plate firmly in place, you should have little trouble getting it right the first time you stencil. One other thing that makes pine such a good stenciling surface is its porosity. Stenciling adheres to it well (sometimes *too* well).

Protecting the Stenciling

If you want to paint a chest, say, before stenciling it, first sand the bare wood well—or refinish and sand the piece if it is old—and apply two coats of flat, oil-based paint. Allow each to dry thoroughly

When stenciling plain or stained wood, the stencil plate must be positioned and stenciled on perfectly the first time; there are no second chances, as there are when stenciling on wood with a light coating of varnish because the paint sinks into the unprotected wood immediately.

The first plate of the three-color stencil pattern is being stenciled onto this cutting board, which was given a light coating of varnish beforehand. A light coat of varnish allows any stenciling mistakes to be wiped off while still wet and restenciled.

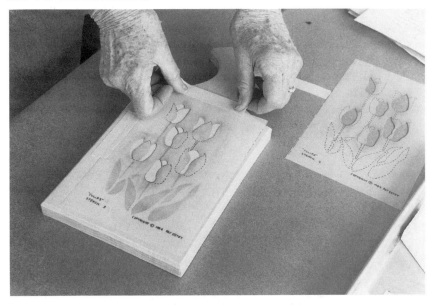

Plate three is securely taped to the wood to ensure precise placement over the first stenciling impressions. It will also help to avoid any mistakes, which would be difficult to remove without damaging the earlier, already dry stenciling. Always be sure to check for unwanted paint on your fingers and on the underside of the stencil plate so none accidentally rubs off on the surface of the wood.

for about 24 hours, and sand lightly between coats. Use japan paint for good coverage on painted surface—textile paint will not adhere to it any more than it will to a glossy wall or other hard surface. If you have trouble getting japan paint to adhere to a surface painted with an oil-based paint, as sometimes happens, lightly rub the area to be stenciled with fine steel wool. For absolute coverage with japan paint on a painted surface, you can use a dull, water-based background paint, but you have to varnish it well to protect it from scratches and nicks. An oil-based background paint is much tougher and is especially good for large pieces of furniture that will receive a lot of use.

If you want to stencil onto a previously stained and varnished piece—in other words, a piece of furniture or other object already in use in your home—first wipe off any wax buildup with denatured alcohol or mineral spirits. If the surface seems too smooth to take the japan paint, rub the area to be stenciled lightly with fine steel wool before stenciling. When the stenciling is dry, you can either wax it, varnish it, or leave it alone if the surface won't receive any real wear or tear. Think about how a piece will be used. Tabletops,

The finished cutting board shows clear, crisp stenciling on a flawless background. A light coating of spray varnishing will protect the stenciling and make the colors more vivid.

stool seats, and bench tops should have a protective coat of varnish or two so the stenciling isn't worn away. The fronts of drawers, paneling, mirror frames, and other vertical surfaces probably won't need much, if any, protection. Also, use your aesthetic judgment. Some pieces will look best with a dull finish, while others will look better with a subtle gleam of varnish or wax. It all depends on your tastes, the style of the piece, and the colors you have chosen as well as the degree of wear the object will receive.

Refinishing Wood

Here are few cautionary words about the "prep work." Always sand bare wood, whether you plan to stencil it as is or finish it first with varnish, stain, or paint. Too-sharp corners on a new piece should be softened, and any splinters or unevenness sanded smooth. An old piece, "taken down", to bare wood should also be sanded well to provide a smooth, flawless surface for the stenciling. Again, when staining raw wood, use a light, penetrating oil-based stain/sealer. Apply the stain sparingly and follow the manufacturer's directions faithfully. Always work in a dust-free area and on a dust-free stenciling surface. Allow stain, varnish, or paint to dry thoroughly between coats and before stenciling. Always allow the stenciling to *dry well* before giving it a brushed-on or sprayed-on coat of varnish. Otherwise it may run or bleed through the varnish.

More stenciling examples from Pat Estey's shop, including stenciled canvas purses, a wooden dipper, two old-fashioned buckets, and another cutting board, this one stenciled with a spot-and-border combination. The tulips on the previous cutting board have been used on one of the buckets.

Apply paint and varnish *thinly*. Be careful to avoid runs, drips, and brush marks. When using spray varnish, go over piece lightly and quickly, and hold the can far enough away from the surface so it doesn't run or "curtain" on the wood. And don't spray too much on or it may take on a whitish cast. Buy good refinishing and finishing products, but buy cheap, disposable paintbrushes. You'll never get them clean anyhow, and it will make your life much easier. Never mind what anyone else says about buying $20 brushes and cleaning them well in turpentine or mineral spirits—it never works.

Stencil Placement

When stenciling (and when painting or varnishing), always try to work on a *horizontal* surface. Turn chests, chairs, and rockers on their backs so the stenciling surface lies flat. Turn shelves, bookcases, and other vertical surfaces on their sides. Place small pieces such as mirror frames flat on a table or the floor.

Depending upon the size of a piece and the size of the stenciling, you may have to measure and mark the surface before stenciling. In most cases, however, you'll probably be able to use the edge of the stencil plate as a guide. When using spot stencils or when centering a border design, use chalk and a measure tape or ruler to center the stenciling, then mark the surface with a cross to indicate where the center of the stenciling plate should be held. The centers of drawers, door panels, chest panels, and other "repetitive" surfaces should be carefully measured and marked so each pattern lines up evenly with the next. Believe me, it will be noticeable if each stencil pattern does not match.

The edges of table and stool tops, mirror frames, panels, chair and rocker backs, and other narrow surfaces provide their own stenciling guides. On small pieces you can usually hold the stencil onto the surface to see how it lines up, how it will look, or how many times it can be stenciled onto the area. You might simply follow the natural lines of a piece with a small border, taking care to stop and start in the same place if you are stenciling legs, the front of a small cabinet, a mirror frame, or other piece with multiple, same-size sections. If you want to produce an overall stenciling design on a large, flat surface, work from the center outward. If you want to create a free-form overall design of large florals, make some paper proofs and arrange these against the surface until it looks right, then mark them off. You should protect extensive stenciling on large pieces with two carefully applied coats of varnish, not paste wax alone.

To measure the center of surfaces for spot stencils, use chalk and a yardstick or ruler to mark an **X** at the center of the surface. Align the center of the stencil where the two lines cross, and tape the plate securely before stenciling. Because of the large number of spaces in this pineapple pattern, it would be safer to tape the plate in place, rather than trying to hold it securely by hand.

A simple pine mirror frame, stained and stenciled with water-based textile paint in a two-color border. Varnish or wax is not necessary to protect the stenciling on objects like this, which will receive little wear.

Stenciling

When you are ready to begin stenciling your well-sanded, stained, or carefully painted—and dust-free—surface, arrange all of your supplies so they are at arm's length. Have everything handy because the stenciling process will go quickly. That is, the paint will dry quickly so you should take great care to measure the surface precisely and cast a keen eye on proportion and color before you begin stenciling.

If you are working on bare or stained wood, give yourself several practice sessions on paper before stenciling the wood. Hold the plate firmly in place on the wood with masking tape or your fingers, and blot the brush off well on folded paper towels until it is *nearly dry*. Stencil in the design in circular shading motions as you did on the paper, moving from the edges of the patterns toward the center. Take care to blot the paint off frequently, especially if you are using

A Pennsylvania Dutch style spot stencil like the one shown here would work well on a variety of large, vertical surfaces, such as the front panels of a large chest, within the panels of a door, or on the front of a tall, narrow cupboard. Traditional designs like these wear well with time and their sharp, almost geometric lines are enhanced with japan paint.

japan paint and thinning it with turpentine. If you want the colors to be stronger, you should add more paint as needed rather than applying it all at once. Remove the stencil plate carefully and position the next plate precisely on top of the first plate before adding the next color.

If you are working on painted or varnished wood, you will have a little more flexibility. If the paint is applied too wet and the stenciling runs or smears, quickly wipe it off with a little turpentine, then a little soap and water, and begin again. Check the edges of your stencil plate for paint buildup periodically, and wipe it off before repositioning the plate on the wood. Once the stenciling is finished, let it dry well and protect it with varnish or wax—or nothing at all.

(Far Left) The chair, rocker, cupboard, hatbox, and two tinware pieces shown here all share similar—but not identical—stenciling colors and patterns that complement one another.

(Left) The simple floral stenciling on this small, white-painted chest seems inspired by the small china box on top, where a portion of the border has been used on the corners of the chest only. The border is repeated again on the lampshade and on the fabric on the floor.

(Bottom Left) A child's room with an unmistakable theme. The train motif has been carried from cloth to wood to paper and to walls.

Stenciling does wonders for the playthings, as well as the serious accessories, of country kids.

Here, a painted pine toy box, canvas carryall, and small canvas floor cloth all carry the same stencil colors and patterns.

Christmas has come around again, this time in three stockings spot-stenciled in soldier, dogs, and angels.

Special holidays make it possible to extend your stenciling creativity. Here, red-and-green stenciling predominates for an unmistakable Christmas theme.

Large, well-spaced spot stencils complement the same pattern in a border stencil at the ceiling and on a chair seat. Large spot stencils, carefully placed, can bring bare walls to life without overpowering the room.

Light and airy lavender, rose, and green border stenciling enlivens butter-colored walls, white baseboard, and curtains. An excellent example of how color, pattern, and style can work together to beautify a room.

A border stencil is cleverly used around a curved window, in the center of a wall, and on the front of cabinets.

Cloth placemats make perfect stenciling surfaces. Here, the two-color pineapple spots in the center are enclosed by two borders of nuts and leaves.

Two cloth wine sacks stenciled with a wood duck spot and a grape spot, both with coordinating borders.

The beauty of flat, opaque stenciling is apparent on this small wooden piece.

Stenciled quilt squares offer plenty of room for a variety of stencil spots using just a few colors for all. The gingham borders around the squares and the border stenciling match the colors in the stenciling.

Large, well-shaded, primitive spot stenciling of a "crazy cat" pattern works nicely with the small, geometric border on this floor cloth's neutral background.

❧ 8 ❧

Stenciling Tinware

PAINTED TINWARE, or toleware, as it is sometimes called, was once bought with a passion by rural housewives. For a small sum they could buy brightly colored trays, cups, pitchers, coffeepots, document boxes, candlesticks, and other tin pieces carted into town by the "tinman" to perk up their kitchens and their spirits. The painted tin was so popular that on days when the itinerant salesman arrived with his wares on village greens, all work stopped. Men and women alike came to see what the peddler had on hand, and the peddler could always count on leaving town with his load considerably lightened.

Tinware was both hand-painted and stenciled, usually on a black lacquered background but often on backgrounds of red and yellow, as well. Large, flat serving trays received the most lavish decorations. Elaborate borders surrounded intricate arrangements of fruits, flowers, and outdoor scenes complete with people and animals. Everything from elegant floral arrangements to primitive barnyard scenes were painted on these trays, which came in several shapes and sizes: flat ovals, rectangles, and octagons, deep-sided coffin-shaped trays and long, narrow bread trays. The larger the piece, it seemed, the more detailed was the artist's painted decoration.

Hinged document boxes (for storing the family's important papers) were often painted with large designs on all four sides and on the top of the lid, with a narrow border around the rim of the lid and at the base of the box. Coffeepots, cannisters, pitchers, and other cylindrical containers might be painted with a large floral or

Old, as well as not-so-old, tinware can still be found at yard sales and antique stores for reasonable prices.

fruit design around the main body and a narrow border around top and bottom rims. Candlesticks, small cups, and match safes were painted or stenciled with a simple, tiny band of curves around an edge, base, or rim. Mugs and small pitchers might have just one pear, apple, or tomato painted with an almost abstract flourish on the side opposite the handle.

Tinware was as much a canvas for early American artisans as were walls, floors, linens, and floor cloths. I suspect that one of the reasons why tinware was produced in so many different shapes and sizes was as much to provide new decorating surfaces as to function as containers for food, drink, candles, and matches.

Buying Tinware

Fortunately, tin and other metals, new and old, are still cheap and plentiful. A hardware store in a town near mine now has a large display case of spanking-new tinware reproductions of the old pieces that are being distributed nationally. They are also reasonably priced, I noticed. Old and new pieces work equally well for stenciling. To find old pieces of tinware, scour yard sales, junk shops, hardware stores, and country auctions for used and new tin kitchenware, lamps, and other items. Pitchers, mugs, cups, plates, scales, buckets, trays, boxes—are waiting to be found, cleaned up, and stenciled.

Consider painting and stenciling a metal bucket or a florist's flower vase. Watering cans are excellent candidates for stenciling, too. Choose pieces that are dent-free, hole-free, and smooth. Rust can be cleaned or sanded off, but a broken or badly pitted piece of tin will try your patience and probably won't be worth the time or money involved.

There is just one caveat when buying old pieces: if it is really old, don't tamper with it. While most valuable, old painted tinware has been taken out of circulation by knowledgeable collectors and dealers (it is valued highly these days), it is just possible that you might come across an old tray or pitcher at a yard sale, the paint barely visible. If you think you have an antique on your hands, play it safe and research it a bit before altering it. You'll be glad you did if it turns out to be worth a couple of hundred dollars.

But there are still plenty of used tin pieces that cost little, and these are the ones worth buying for a few dollars or more for stenciling. Never pay more than you are comfortable parting with. Stenciling will be less fun if you have to worry about getting your fifteen-dollar tinware investment perfect.

Preparing the Tinware

To stencil an old piece of tinware, one with traces of old and faded paints, remove all of the paint with a commercial paint stripper. This is easy to do. Just take two or three pieces of coarse steel wool (be sure to wear gloves) and go over the piece until all of the paint is removed. Get the metal as clean and smooth as you possibly can because you'll be giving it six coats of paint and a final wax finish. Any chips, cracks, or dents will be magnified on an otherwise smoothly finished surface, so take the time to take off any rough spots. If the metal is paint-free but rusted or pitted, go over it with rust remover and sand it smooth with fine sandpaper. Wash the piece well in soap and water to remove any traces of remover or dirt, and dry it thoroughly.

Now give the tin two coats of metal primer to prevent future rust and give the background paint a good surface on which to adhere. Allow each coat of primer to dry for a full 24 hours—never skimp on the time—sanding lightly between and after coats. Rub the final coat of primer down with fine steel wool to roughen the surface a bit for the background paint and to remove any stray brush marks. Try to keep the surface and any projections such as handles and spouts as smooth as you can so the final surface shows no lumps, drips, or ridges that might detract from the stenciling.

After you've rubbed the metal primer down with steel wool, add the first of two coats of background paint. Use a flat, oil-based paint in any color you like. Black, red, and yellow are the traditional

A metal mailbox makes an ideal subject for stenciling with japan paint.

background colors for stenciled tinware, but since you'll be using japan paint, you can choose any background color you like. A creamy white background will work well with blue, green, and red stenciling. A dark blue or dull green background will contrast beautifully with gold or silver stenciling.

Applying Background

Using a narrow paintbrush, apply the background paint along the general direction of the lines of the piece. Paint tall, cylindrical pitchers, pots, mugs and buckets from top to bottom. Paint trays and other flat objects from side to side. Use long strokes along long edges. Try to leave as few brush strokes on the surface as possible, and paint on the thinnest coat you can manage. Don't let the paint become thick in tight places around handles, spouts, and rims. If you are painting a tray, paint one side at a time. When the first background coat has dried thoroughly, sand it lightly and hold it to the light to see if the surface is smooth and dust-free before adding the second coat of paint. Rub the second coat down with fine steel wool and you'll be ready to stencil.

Stenciling

As always, have all of your stenciling supplies handy. Measure and mark the piece off if necessary, especially if it is a large tray or other piece with a spacious surface. Give some thought to how you want the stenciling to appear on round, broad surfaces. Do you want it to wrap around the entire surface or cover only one or both sides of the object? Where will the stenciling appear in relation to handles, spouts, or other projections? Will you use a border-and-spot or just one of them alone? Think your stenciling plan through, holding the plates against the surface of the tin in a variety of ways until it fits and looks just right. If a border stencil proves to be too tight a fit on a small piece, trim the plate off until it fits onto the surface of the tinware comfortably. Once you know where you want to place the stencil, hold it firmly in place with masking tape or your fingers when stenciling.

Getting the right paint consistency on tin can be difficult because the metal is so hard and smooth. Try some proofs, playing around with different proportions of paint and turpentine. Pay less attention to shading and more to producing nice, sharp outlines so that the stenciling almost appears to "float" on the surface of the painted tinware. Be generous with the paint, but add it a little at a time so it does not run beneath the stencil pattern. Unlike stenciling on wood and fabric, "thicker is better" on tinware, and any mistakes you make while stenciling can be wiped off completely before restenciling.

Protecting the Stenciling

Once the piece is stenciled, allow the stenciling to dry for 2 or 3 days before applying the first coat of varnish. If you don't allow the stencil paint to dry, it may liquefy beneath the varnish, which is meant to seal, protect, and emphasize the stenciling, not obliterate it. After the first coat of varnish has dried (for 24 hours), rub it down lightly but well with fine steel wool and apply the second coat of varnish. Paint the two coats of varnish on as carefully as you did the background color, allowing for few brush marks and no drips or buildup. If necessary, rub down any brush marks that show up after the final coat of varnish dries before giving the piece a coat of hard, clear paste wax for a warm, soft sheen.

Considering all of the steps involved in stenciling tinware—removing any rust, sanding the bare tin, applying two coats of metal primer, painting on the stenciling, applying two coats of varnish, and applying a final coat of paste wax—you may want to stencil several pieces of tinware at one time. As the metal primer on the first piece dries, you can begin work on the second piece. As that piece dries, you can brush on the background color of the first piece, and so on, working on three or more pieces of tinware on different days. If you coordinate your stenciling colors and patterns carefully, you can even produce a matched set of tinware to display on a small set of hanging shelves, painted or stenciled, or course, to match the tinware.

❧ 9 ❧

Stenciling
Fabric & Paper

cAS SOMETIMES HAPPENS in both life and in stenciling, we have managed to work our way back to the beginning. This chapter describes what I think are the two easiest surfaces to stencil: fabric and paper. After climbing up walls, crawling on floors, bending over furniture, and grasping slippery tinware, you have come to a couple of surfaces that possess all the right qualities for easy, mistake-proof stenciling. Both fabric and paper are a cinch to stencil: you simply lay them on the table and let the paints, brushes, and stencils do all the work.

Well, it's not quite that easy; but it is a whole lot simpler than stenciling other surfaces, mostly because water-based, easy-to-clean-up textile paint is used exclusively on these two surfaces. The key to successful stenciling on paper and fabric is a brush that you could swear is absolutely dry. The "dry-brush rule" eliminates absolutely all guesswork about how much paint is too much on fabric and paper. And the paint that is used on these surfaces goes on straight from the container, or is mixed together for custom shades right on a saucer. There is no experimentation with turpentine-and-paint mixtures for the right consistency. The consistency you find in the jar of textile paint is the one you will work with. And when the stenciling is done, you simply wash all of your tools, your hands, and anything else that comes into contact with the paint with soap and water.

Fabric

Textile paint produces beautiful, crisp stenciling that is easy to shade, darken, and duplicate endlessly. Unlike japan paint, it is easy to produce the same tone and shading with any number of stenciling impressions because the consistency of the paint does not have to be fiddled with again and again. Textile paint produces beautiful stenciling on smooth, dull fabrics such as cotton and muslin, as well as on synthetic blends. It should not be used on wools or other "nubby" fabrics because it is hard to stencil smoothly on these fabrics. But once textile paint is stenciled onto other fabrics, it remains there permanently, wash after wash.

Stenciled fabric projects go on and on. Unlike stenciling permanent fixtures such as walls, floors, and furniture, you need not worry about how much stenciling is too much, or whether two kind of designs and various color schemes go together. After all, curtains and bedspreads can be stored away and sheets changed while different ones are brought out and stenciled in another pattern-and-color scheme.

Curtains, bed linens, and wall stenciling can be coordinated to match one another, as can tablecloths, napkins, place mats, and aprons. You can also stencil rugs and window shades, handkerchiefs, shirt pockets, socks, T-shirts, sweatshirts, skirts,

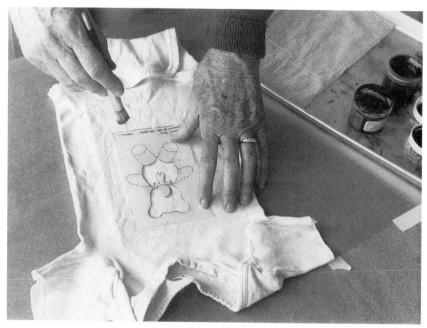

Plain, flat cotton fabrics of all kinds can be stenciled easily with water-based textile paint—the only paint that should ever be used on fabric. Here, Pat Estey stencils on the body of a teddy bear on this infant's T-shirt.

The hems of curtains and other large, square pieces of fabric make perfect guides for border stencils. Here, the tie-back comes into good service, as well. The floral border flows naturally around the corners of the curtain panel, making this one of the easiest fabric stencil projects you can do.

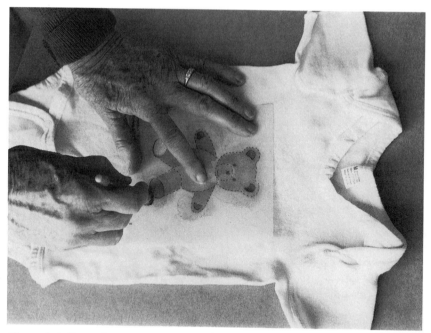

Here, details such as paws, eyes, and ears are stenciled onto the teddy bear pattern.

scarves, quilt squares, wall hangings, and potholders. Almost any fabric but wool and very loose weaves will take stenciling, but the easiest to stencil are those fabrics that are light colored, smooth, and finely woven.

Colors and Patterns

Stenciling schemes include everything from the tiniest border of flowers or geometrics on the hem of a handkerchief to a row of 5-inch-high geese on the hem of a bed sheet. As with other surfaces, portions of a large design can be used to accent a hem while the large part of the pattern is stenciled in the center of the fabric. You can use as many or as few colors as you like, of course, and the colors and patterns you choose for fabrics can just as easily be coordinated with existing stenciling on walls, floors, and furniture. As you did with those surfaces, keep the colors and style of the existing room in mind when choosing stenciling schemes for curtains, bed linens, and table linens—unless you are stenciling table linens or other items for use outdoors or in a room without existing stenciling.

When stenciling table linens, keep the patterns and colors of china and other table or kitchenware in mind. If you give it all a bit of thought and time, even custom-mixing your textile paints to match a particular shade of color in your dishes, you can produce a coordinated color-and-pattern scheme impossible to put together from store-bought merchandise.

Fabrics are remarkably easy to measure for stenciling. Sheets, curtains, pillowcases, tablecloths, and other square items have natural borders and clear-cut centers. Pockets, sleeves, collars, and skirt hems also make logical stenciling areas for spots and borders. As I said earlier, stenciling shows up best on light-colored fabrics, not only because light backgrounds provide good contrast for the paint but because dark fabrics require too much paint to produce enough contrast between the stenciling and the background of the fabric. The result would be a thick, stiff stenciling that would be a little uncomfortable for wear or use.

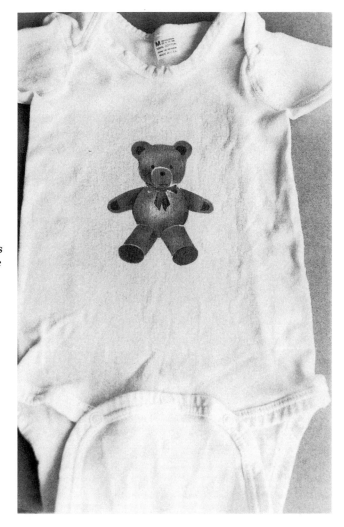

The finished bear. Small pieces of clothing such as this infant's T-shirt make excellent ''handmade'' gifts.

Even frequently washed fabrics such as dishtowels can be stenciled with textile paint and retain the stenciling wash after wash.

Shading on fabric is easy and comes naturally. In fact, all fabric stenciling—as well as paper stenciling—*should* be shaded to give the stenciling a translucent, barely-there look. The transparent property of textile paint shouldn't be wasted on any surface, but especially not on fabric.

To stencil a piece of fabric—a sheet, for example—place it flat on a large table or an ironing board, and tack it down or tape it securely to hold the section to be stenciled taut and flat. If the fabric is wrinkled or shifts at all as you stencil it, the stenciling will not reproduce well. There may be gaps of white in the impression or, once the fabric is flattened out, the stenciling may not resemble the stencil pattern very much at all. If you want to stencil a large

The completed two-color floral border on a simple cotton dishtowel —another good gift idea.

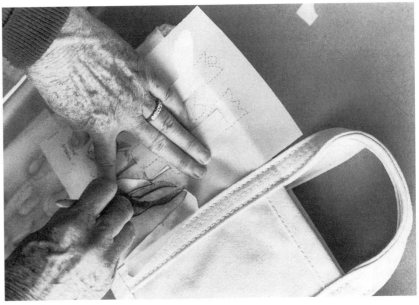

Here, Pat Estey stencils the same tulip stencil pattern used on the cutting board onto a canvas tote bag. A single stencil pattern goes a long way. You can use this pattern on countless types of surfaces, in different color combinations, using either japan paint or textile paint.

The finished canvas tote bag. A small border of a different pattern, with the same colors, has been used to complement the large tulip pattern, which would not fit inside the center panel. Mixing patterns is one way to customize your stenciling projects.

stencil pattern onto the center of a sheet, tack the ends of the sheet below the table to help keep the center of the fabric taut. Or fold the sheet in thirds and securely tape the top and bottom ends to the table. Do anything, in fact, that keeps the fabric immovable and flat as you work. When stenciling something two-sided such as a pillowcase, slip a piece of cardboard or blotting paper inside the case so the stencil paint does not soak through to the other side.

Place measuring guides for borders or spots with chalk, masking tape, or an ironed-in crease. If you want to experiment with an overall free-form design, place cutout paper proofs on the fabric at random until you find an arrangement you like, and lightly mark the fabric where the patterns will be stenciled on. Wash your hands well before stenciling, and keep a damp towel handy to clean your fingers as you work. Remember: when the textile paint touches the fabric, it's there to stay.

Now assemble your supplies—not much, just the paint, brush, stencil plate, paper towel, and damp cloth. Check to see that the fabric is taut, then hold the stencil plate down firmly with your fingers on either side of the pattern opening. Tip the very ends of the brush bristles into the paint, and wipe it off on a paper towel as though you were trying to get rid of all the paint. Apply the paint in circular, shading motions, working from the outside edges of the pattern toward the center. If you want a little more coverage, add a very small amount of paint at a time so it does not visibly thicken on the fabric. Go slowly and carefully, staying mindful of how you are shading each repeat pattern so they all match, and you will produce clear, well-defined stenciling. Keep your eye on the paint at all times to make sure none gets on the underside of the stencil, on your fingertips, or anywhere else where it might accidentally get on the fabric.

When you finish stenciling, wait 15 or 20 minutes and then iron each side of the fabric with a *dry* iron for 10 to 15 minutes in order to "set" the stenciling permanently. That's it. You can use the fabric and wash it as you would any other fabric, and the stenciling will not fade or run. If it does fade after repeated washings, you can reapply the stenciling and reset it again with a hot iron.

Paper

The final stenciling surface is the easiest. I can't imagine a cheaper and faster (or more prolific) stenciling surface for the beginner to try her hand on. If you have read this far and haven't decided what you want to stencil first, consider buying some inexpensive plain, light-colored stationery, a couple of small stencils (either spots or borders, or both, will be fine), some textile paints, two or three brushes, and get to work stenciling the tops and edges of the stationery as well as the back flap of the envelopes.

In addition to designing your own writing paper and envelopes, you can stencil gift boxes, shopping bags, file folders, book covers, blotter paper (sprayed with a light coat of varnish first to keep the stenciling from sinking into the paper), address-book covers, and other paper accessories at little or no risk.

If paper is the perfect surface to flex your stenciling fingers on, it is also the perfect way to introduce children to the craft. Kids happen to like crafts of all kinds, but they tend to have a more casual idea of the notion of "perfection" than we do. So a craft that is inexpensive and relatively mess-free like stenciling paper is a good way to keep them busy on rainy afternoons. A little stenciling kit of brushes, textile paints, stencil plates, and plain stationery and envelopes will make a fine gift for older kids.

Paper will allow you to acquire a feel for the very same stenciling techniques—how to hold the brush, register stencil plates, and apply and shade the stencil paints—that you will use later on more permanent surfaces such as walls, floors, furniture, and fabrics without any great loss should you produce less-than-satisfactory results the first few times. Paper stenciling is also a handy way to prepare a variety of different paper proofs to use as

Canadians like stenciling, too. This abstract spot stencil was found in a farmhouse in Stirling, Ontario.

guides when approaching complicated wall and floor stenciling projects. You might practice large, multicolored spot stencils in different color combinations and styles with an eye toward using them on walls and other surfaces, or string together several "pages" of border patterns to give yourself a preview of the large, elaborate stenciling you eventually want to try around the tops of the dining room or bedroom walls.

Paper stenciling will give you a risk-proof feel for the wealth of stenciling patterns and color combinations that you can try on those plain surfaces in your house which, until now, have resisted all other decorative efforts.

❤❦ 10 ❧❤

Stenciling
a Nursery

EACH YEAR, thousands of dens, studies, guest rooms, and other small, little-used rooms are emptied of their hodgepodge of furnishings—usually the stuff that is unwanted anywhere else in the house—and given new life, figuratively and literally. New curtains, fresh paint, and a few simple pieces of furniture (much of it borrowed and of different vintage, color, and condition) are all that may make up the new decor. While framed Mother Goose prints and other purely decorative items might make the room more inviting for parents and baby alike, the bare essentials such as crib, bedding, changing table, toys and other supplies for the new baby often strain the baby budget to its limit. Precious little may be left over after the new parents have spent upwards of a hundred dollars on toys alone.

Benefits

Stenciling can transform a plain, small room into a storybook nursery with themes and motifs that grow from your own imagination, not those already printed on fabrics, paper, and wood. Since the nursery will probably receive a fresh coat of paint and new curtains before you stencil, you can choose a flat, light-colored paint that will take water-based textile stencil paints. These will make stenciling easier, of course, and will produce a softer-looking stenciling than japan paint would. You will also want to match the wall stenciling to curtains and crib bedding—sheets, pillows, coverlet, and bolsters—using the same kind of paint to produce the

A lively border of bears, rocking horses, and balloons make this room unmistakably "baby's room." Rockers for the rocking horse and facial features for the bears will be added with another stencil plate and color. Here, the balloons are being stenciled on.

While it is easier to stencil borders using border stencils, this mother-to-be has chosen to use spot stencils in order to produce just the design she wanted for her nursery. Simple, primitive spots like these, when measured by eye, produce a slightly "off-kilter" border that can be charming.

same soft shades. Textile paint will allow you to more easily duplicate and coordinate stenciling colors and patterns on every surface in the room, except for floors and furniture with a glossy finish.

Selecting Patterns and Colors

Nursery stenciling patterns and colors are as varied as nursery rhymes and all the themes associated with babies. A friend awaiting her first baby transformed a small guest room in her house with her own idea of the images of innocence. She stenciled the nursery's walls with a ceiling border of alternating teddy bears, rocking horses, and balloons. A portion of that pattern was picked up on the white cotton curtains at the windows, and another portion was used to dress up the bedding in the crib. Later on, she found small toys, wooden wall plaques, and other accessories that matched the teddy bear-rocking horse-balloon theme, and by the time Hayley had arrived, her room was already occupied by the loving creative touches of Mother's own hands.

To decorate a baby's room with stenciling, use your own childhood preferences as a guide. Select stenciling themes from favorite toys and nursery rhymes when you were little so that you, as well as the baby, can enjoy the playful imagery stenciled on walls, fabrics, and furniture.

The finished nursery, stenciled in a theme and colors that the mother hopes the baby will also find appealing. Elements of the ceiling border have been picked up on the mirror frame, the white curtains, the small mobile, and the wooden toy on the dresser.

Supply Sources

GOOD STENCILING SUPPLIES can be found in special shops and housewares' departments of larger stores almost everywhere these days. If you can't find a stencil shop in your neighborhood, try shopping for paints, brushes, and stencil plates in department stores, wood shops, craft stores, and the craft sections of large discount and drug stores. Look for shops that carry a wide selection of both japan and textile paints, brushes, and plates, as well as stenciled objects to fuel your imagination. Stencil shops that specialize in the products of large manufacturers such as Adele Bishop and Stencil-Ease often offer stenciling classes where beginners can pick up valuable ideas and first-hand stenciling tips.

Sandpaper, steel wool, turpentine, mineral spirits, paints and varnish removers, paste wax, paintbrushes, and other furniture-refinishing supplies are available at all hardware stores, discount stores, or home supply stores. My favorite refinishing supplies are made by Minwax, Parks, and Red Devil. All are reliable and do a great job. If you have any trouble locating the name of a canvas supplier in your telephone directory, try looking under businesses that might use or sell canvas in the normal course of their work: upholsterers, artists' suppliers, awning, canopy, and tentmakers, and sailmakers or ship chandlers.

A stenciler's library. Books, magazines, and other printed sources provide a wealth of good ideas for stenciling on furniture, walls, tinware, fabric, floors, and other surfaces.

Index

About the Author

Wanda Shipman has both written and edited books and magazine articles about such homegrown American crafts as stenciling, rug-hooking, chair-caning, candle-making, ice-cream making, gardening, cooking, and homebuilding. She lives with her husband and three cats in southern Vermont.

Other Bestsellers From TAB

☐ **YEAR-ROUND CRAFTS FOR KIDS—Barbara L. Dondiego, Illustrated by Jacqueline Cawley**

Easy to use, the handy month-by-month format provides a year of inspiring projects, many focused on seasonal themes to ensure young children's enthusiasm. Valentines, paper airplanes, and cookies for Easter, paper bag bunny puppets, string painting, Hanukkah candles and gingerbread boys, bell and candle mobiles and of course Christmas trees for December are just a few of the fun things to make. 256 pp., 180 illus., plus 8 pages of color.

Paper $15.95   **Hard $19.95**
Book No. 2904

☐ **MAKING MOVABLE WOODEN TOYS—Alan and Gill Bridgewater**

This book contains 20 toy projects that will challenge and excite the creative woodworker in you. Fro Russian nesting dolls to an American folk art baby rattle, traditional pull-along toys to English soldiers, these are the toys adults enjoy making and children enjoy playing with! The designs employ whittling and lathe work among other techniques. Precise, over-the-shoulder instructions and numerous work-in-progress illustrations guide you through every step of construction. 240 pp., 106 illus.

Paper $18.95   **Hard $23.95**
Book No. 3079

☐ **WOODCRAFTING HERITAGE TOYS: A TREASURY OF CLASSIC PROJECTS—H. LeRoy Marlow**

This classic treasury is for the woodworker who wants projects demanding more skill and artistry than the ordinary quick-and-easy plans found in most books. It is a collection of 17 delightful and *original* keepsake-quality wooden toys. All the toys presented are made entirely of wood fastened by glue—no nails, screws, staples, plastic, or other materials are used. Full-scale patterns for the toys need only to be traced—no enlargements or other calculations are necessary. 192 pp., 167 illus., plus 8 full-color pages.

Paper $19.95   **Hard $24.95**
Book No. 2863

☐ **STRIP QUILTING—Diane Wold**

Diane Wold is an expert quilt-maker and her enthusiasm for the art of strip quilting is contagious. After introducing you to the tools, fabrics, techniques, and sewing methods used in strip quilting, she covers all the steps needed to complete a finished project including making borders, backing, using batting, basting, doing the actual quilting, and binding. You'll also find directions for using different types of patterns—multiple bands, one-band shifted patterns, and more. 184 pp., 165 illus. with 8 Full-Color Pages.

Paper $15.95   **Hard $21.95**
Book No. 2822

☐ **MARIONETTE MAGIC: FROM CONCEPT TO CURTAIN CALL—Bruce Taylor, Illustrations by Cathy Stubington and Bruce Taylor**

Puppets are fun weekend projects and offer a welcomechallenge to the woodworker who is seeking a change of pace. Requiring no prior puppet-making experience, this book provides a complete apprenticeship in puppet-making, as well as a concise course in staging. Taylor describes how you can transform wood, plaster, and papier-mache into animated figures. Complete plans and detailed instructions are accompanied by tips and tricks of the trade. 176 pp. 143 illus.

Paper $15.95   **Hard $19.95**
Book No. 3091

☐ **FRAMES AND FRAMING: THE ULTIMATE ILLUSTRATED HOW-TO-DO-IT GUIDE—Gerald F. Laird and Louise Meiere Dunn, CPF**

This illustrated step-by-step guide gives complete instructions and helpful illustrations on how to cut mats, choose materials, and achieve attractively framed art. Filled with photographs and eight pages of full color, this book shows why a frame's purpose is to enhance, support, and protect the artwork, and never call attention to itself. You can learn how to make a beautiful frame that complements artwork. 208 pp., 264 illus., 8 pages full color.

Paper $15.95   **Hard $19.95**
Book No. 2909

Other Bestsellers From TAB

☐ **A MASTER CARVER'S LEGACY—essentials of wood carving techniques—Brieuc Bouché**

Expert guidance on the basics of wood carving from a master craftsman with over 50 years experience. All the techniques for making a whole range of woodcarved items are included. You'll learn how-to's for basic chip carving, the basic rose, cutting of twinings, a classic acanthus leaf, and a simple carving in the round. In no time at all you will be making many of the projects featured. 176 pp., 135 illus., 8 1/2″ × 11″.

Paper $17.95   **Hard $24.95**
Book No. 2629

☐ **MAKING POTPOURRI, COLOGNES AND SOAPS—102 NATURAL RECIPES—David A. Webb**

Fill your home with the scents of spring—all year long! This down-to-earth guide reintroduces the almost forgotten art of home crafts. You'll learn how to use simple ingredients (flowers, fruits, spices, and herbs) to make a variety of useful scented products, from soaps and deodorant to potpourris and colognes. Webb demystifies this age-old craft and offers step-by-step diagrams, work-in-progress photographs, and easy-to-follow recipes to give you everything you need to successfully create your own home crafts. 144 pp., 98 illus.

Paper $12.95   **Hard $14.95**
Book No. 2918

☐ **DESIGNING AND CONSTRUCTING MOBILES —Jack Wiley**

Discover the fun and satisfaction of learning to create exciting mobile art forms . . . to add a personal decorator touch to your home, as unique craft projects for a school class or club, even as a new income source! All the skills and techniques are here for the taking in this excellent, step-by-step guide to designing and constructing mobiles from paper, wood, metals, plastic, and other materials. 224 pp., 281 illus.

Paper $14.95   **Hard $19.95**
Book No. 1839

☐ **BUILD YOUR OWN GRANDFATHER CLOCK AND SAVE—John A. Nelson**

Thorough and exact plans make this challenging project achievable by woodworkers of all skill levels. The design is an adaptation of two or three clocks made by 18th-century clockmaker Nathaniel Mulliken. Every aspect of construction is covered, from building the case and hood to installing premade movements. Nelson even details how to make your own brass hinges and escutcheons from scratch. Many illustrations complement the step-by-step instructions. 144 pp., 99 illus.

Paper $15.95   **Hard $19.95**
Book No. 3053

☐ **CRAFTS FOR KIDS: A Month-By-Month Idea Book—Barbara L. Dondiego**

Creative and educational crafts for small children designed by a professional! More than 160 craft and cooking projects that can be made easily and inexpensively, from readily available materials! Step-by-step instructions plus exceptional illustrations enhance each project which are arranged by months to take advantage of special seasonal occasions! 224 pp., 156 illus.

Paper $13.95   **Hard $17.95**
Book No. 1784

☐ **GUNSMITHING FUNDAMENTALS—A GUIDE FOR PROFESSIONAL RESULTS—Franklin Fry**

Hunters, gun collectors, antique gun enthusiasts, and target shooters will all want this book. It's a one-stop source on the fundamentals of professional gunsmithing. Including everything from tips on how to purchase a used firearm to professional techniques for refinishing and refurbishing all types of guns including: automatic pistols, single shots, double shots, and over/unders, pump and automatic shotguns, and all types of rifles. 176 pp., 91 illus.

Paper $14.95   **Hard $17.95**
Book No. 2932

Other Bestsellers From TAB

A-1